NASHVILLE TALES

Also by Louise Littleton Davis

Frontier Tales of Tennessee
More Tales of Tennessee

NASHVILLE TALES

TALES

LOUISE LITTLETON DAVIS

PELICAN PUBLISHING COMPANY

GRETNA 1982

First printing, November 1981
Second printing, January 1982

Library of Congress Cataloging in Publication Data

Davis, Louise Littleton.
  Nashville tales.

  Bibliography: p.
  Includes index.
  1. Nashville (Tenn.)—History—Addresses, essays,
lectures. I. Title.
F444.N245D38   976.8'55   81-13778
ISBN 0-88289-294-0   AACR2

Manufactured in the United States of America

Published by Pelican Publishing Company, Inc.
1101 Monroe Street, Gretna, Louisiana 70053

Contents

Acknowledgments

To John Seigenthaler, president, editor, and publisher of *The Tennessean,* for permission to publish these stories, all of which appeared originally in *The Sunday Magazine* of *The Tennessean* or the *Panorama* section of that paper.

To the entire staff of the manuscript section of the Tennessee State Library and Archives for their assistance in my search for much of the material.

To the entire staff of The Nashville Room of the Public Library of Nashville and Davidson County for their aid in my search for material.

To countless staff members of the Metropolitan Government of Nashville and Davidson County, who have helped trace deeds and land grants, wills and household sales. That includes particularly the office of register of deeds, with much work by Jim Allen.

To the late Stanley F. Horn, for his vast knowledge and enthusiastic assistance in establishing much of Nashville history. To Mrs. Roy C. Avery, for her wealth of genealogical material.

To Harriet C. Owsley, former coeditor of the Andrew Jackson Papers, for her help in directing me to little-known sources for many of these stories.

To Cecil L. Sanford Jr. and the Hillsborough Historical Society of Hillsborough, North Carolina, and to the Orange County Public Library in Hillsborough for assisting me in researching the story on Gen. Francis Nash.

To Dr. Chalmers G. Davidson, of Davidson College, Davidson, North Carolina, for aid in researching the story on Gen. William Lee Davidson of Davidson, North Carolina.

Preface

From Gen. Francis Nash who moved from Virginia to seek his fortune in North Carolina in 1763 and Gen. William Lee Davidson who left Pennsylvania as a child about 1748 to become "the most completely adored man in North Carolina," Nashville and Davidson County took their names. And these two men who gave their lives in Revolutionary War battles tie this region to the nation's founding.

For no state in the South has had a more varied impact on the nation's history than Tennessee, with its three presidents—Andrew Jackson, James K. Polk, and Andrew Johnson—who presided over such divergent eras of warfare and conquest. And no city within Tennessee has so strongly shaped the state's development as Nashville has.

Thus this collection, *Nashville Tales,* seems the natural outgrowth of two earlier volumes, *Frontier Tales of Tennessee* (published in 1976) and *More Tales of Tennessee* (published in 1978). All three are collections of stories that had been published in *The Sunday Tennessean Magazine* or the *Panorama* section of *The Tennessean,* and all the stories in this third volume are aimed at giving readers an intimate view of some of the moments and men who converged to make Nashville a tapestry of courage and color.

From the day James Robertson announced that marauding Indians who murdered his sons would not chase him from the Nashborough fort he had founded, until the last days of his life—spent among the Indians, trying to see that they were treated fairly by the white man—the complexity of the frontier was apparent.

Even venturesome Indian fighter John Rains, who protected early settlers from warring red men, settled down into solid farm life and lived in comfort and even luxury in his last years. His life bridged the gap between frontier terror and quiet prosperity.

And Dr. John Shelby, born in perilous conditions in neighboring Sumner County, added immeasurably to Nashville's social, educational, and professional life after he brought home his M.D. degree from the University of Pennsylvania and his bride from fashionable Philadelphia.

But he, like the rest of the medical profession, had his hands tied when epidemics struck in the days before vaccinations and effective drugs. Hundreds of lives were lost here, for instance, when cholera left the city helpless.

All of Nashville suffered for three years during the Civil War when the Union Army occupied the city, and a crucial showdown between North and South came in the Battle of Nashville on December 15 and 16, 1864. In that contest for control of railroads and steamboats that delivered men and supplies to the Union Army, Nashville hills echoed with gunfire for two days, and icy battlefields ran red with the blood of barefoot soldiers.

Little more than 30 years later the city had recovered sufficiently from the grim Reconstruction years to host Nashville's biggest party—a six-month celebration of Tennessee's 100th birthday. The impact of that celebration is strongly felt in Nashville civic and social life today.

These and other stories are compiled in the hope that they will bring readers an insight into some of the triumphs and tribulations, the high courage and joyous adventure that have formed the city of Nashville.

NASHVILLE TALES

Gen. Francis Nash
Gave the City His Name

The exuberant Francis Nash, when he arrived in Hillsborough, North Carolina, near his twenty-first birthday, was so human, so handsome, so full of plans in business and law and politics, that no one has been able to sort all of them out.

There were romances, sad and joyful. And there were fierce stands to take, and honors and embarrassments—in both public and private life.

The fact that Nashville, Tennessee, and Nash County, North Carolina, were named in his honor shortly after the young man's death over two hundred years ago is some measure of his hold on the affection of his home state and the new nation.

The fact that a plaque honoring him was unveiled recently at the United States Military Academy at West Point indicates new interest in that charmed life. And Nash seems close when one stands in the graceful parlor of the tall frame "mansion house" he built on a choice site in Hillsborough in 1772. The lawns where he walked, the boxwood-bordered circular drive where he used to dash up on the fine horses he loved, are reminders of the elegance he enjoyed.

On a recent visit to Hillsborough—that cradle of Middle Tennessee—I retraced the scenes where Nash took part in some of the most dramatic action in this country's struggle for freedom.

3

Just to enter Hillsborough—where, in many ways, Nash-ville had its beginning—is to step back over two hundred years in history. Located in the piedmont area of North Carolina, about twelve miles from the University of North Carolina at Chapel Hill, and about twelve miles from Duke University at Durham, Hillsborough has been so powerful in both pre–Revolution and post–Revolution North Carolina that it was long considered the logical location for the capital.

The names of the place and its streets tell of its ancient ties. Hillsborough itself was named for the Earl of Hills-borough, British secretary of state for the colonies under George III. And Hillsborough is county seat for Orange County, so named to honor William III, of the House of Orange, ruler of England from 1689 to 1702.

The names of Hillsborough streets, where Lord Corn-wallis paraded his troops and freedom-loving men defied them, echo the era: King Street, a main thoroughfare run-ning west to east and once the scene of angry demonstra-tions for justice; Queen Street, a quiet way of handsome homes; Tryon Street, named for one of the influential colo-nial governors, and more.

But when aristocratic Nash rode into Hillsborough in 1763 to make his home, it was still a backwoods town of log houses and taverns, and a small frame courthouse stood on the same spot where the 1844 courthouse stands today.

Nash, born in 1742 at his father's Templeton Manor plantation in Prince Edward County, Virginia, was fourth son of the wealthy John Nash, a power in Virginia govern-ment and education. John Nash, in turn, had come to this country from his native Wales after marrying Anne, daugh-ter of Sir Hugh Owen, of equally distinguished Welsh fam-ily.

Francis Nash was the youngest of the four sons, and he had apparently come to Hillsborough along with his older brother, Abner Nash—a lawyer who was to become governor of North Carolina. Abner Nash was in fact governor when the first settlers arrived on the Cumberland to found what is now Nashville.

And Abner Nash was so highly regarded in national affairs that his death in 1786 at age forty-three, while he was serving in Congress (then seated in New York), was occasion for one of the memorable funeral processions of that era. Not only did the cabinet and the supreme court attend the services at St. Paul's Church, but most of the ambassadors from Europe were also there.

It was Abner as well as Francis Nash who bought a great deal of property in Hillsborough, and operated a mill down by the little Eno River that runs by the town. Young Francis Nash—affable, trained as a lawyer, graceful in manner— rose quickly in public office and was soon appointed to one of the most lucrative jobs in the colonies: clerk to the Superior Court of Orange County.

As it turned out, that job put him under suspicion from small farmers who were brutally oppressed by every county officeholder from sheriff to register. And the fact that he was law partner and friend to Edmund Fanning, county register and most hated man in Orange, turned suspicious eyes toward Nash.

Fanning, a native New Yorker and Yale graduate whose arrogant way of crushing farmers to fill his own pocket fanned the fires of revolution, somehow maintained his friendship with Nash for a while.

Fanning's lavish living, the fine home he built on King Street, across the street from where the 200-year-old Colonial Inn stands today, incensed farmers struggling to pay their taxes.

Orange County then included what is now five more counties and parts of six others, and farmers from that vast territory organized themselves into a powerful group they called the "Regulators." After long efforts at justice, mobs of them crowded into the courtroom in Hillsborough on September 24, 1768, and literally beat up and chased out of the courthouse every officeholder from sheriff to register and every lawyer in the building.

Judge Richard Henderson, who was later to organize the first band of settlers to come west and settle what is now Nashville, was presiding over court that morning, and he escaped the mob only because he promised to hold court until the end of the term. (He broke that promise, and the Regulators later burned his home and stable to the ground.)

But the mob in the courtroom made a lunge for the hated Fanning, and when he darted to the judge's bench for protection, they dragged him out by the heels and mauled him with clubs until he wrestled loose and fled to a nearby store. There they broke the windows and pounded him with stones.

They burned Fanning's house and all his belongings. Eventually Fanning went to England to make his home. Nash escaped the courthouse mob in all of the confusion, and when an investigation of wrongdoing was made, he was found not guilty.

When Governor Tryon ordered the militia to Hillsborough to quell the Regulators, Capt. Francis Nash was chosen to command the Hillsborough militiamen. And when the showdown came at the Battle of the Alamance on May 16, 1771, the poorly equipped Regulators were soundly defeated.

But there were brave men fighting there, and when six of the survivors were hanged for their part in the uprising, local patriots were haunted by the words of one of the men, just before the noose was fitted around his neck: "The blood that we have shed will be as good seed sown in good ground, which will soon reap a hundredfold."

Out of that discontent, a great migration westward took shape. Richard Henderson, ruined in Hillsborough, negotiated with the Indians to buy much of the territory that is now Kentucky and Tennessee. He engaged Daniel Boone and James Robertson to lead parties westward to settle the new land.

And Henderson, who eventually set up a real estate office near Nashville and drew up the Cumberland Compact to govern this area, was apparently the man who named the little fort on the Cumberland for his good friend in Hillsborough, Francis Nash.

For Nash, the man for whom Nashville was named, had died a popular hero on George Washington's staff long before the Nashville area was settled.

There was no conflict, in his mind, in his fighting against the Regulators at the Battle of the Alamance and against the British oppression during the Revolution. At the Alamance, he was fighting against lawlessness and terrorism, as he saw it. In the Revolution, he was fighting for freedom for all Americans.

Few of his private papers are left, and of those remaining most concern military movements during the Revolutionary War. But it is known that he married in 1770, in the midst of the Regulator troubles, and that marriage allied him with one of the prominent families of North Carolina.

His bride, Sarah Moore, was daughter of Judge Maurice Moore of Wilmington, North Carolina, and sister of Supreme Court Justice Alfred Moore. When Nash was courting Sarah, he wrote a friend, asking if he could borrow a fine horse that matched Nash's own mount. He wanted to impress the girl with the matching pair. But courtship was no problem for Francis Nash, described by friends as "handsome in person, easy and graceful and gentle in manners, energetic and thorough in all that he undertook."

Known as a builder in Hillsborough, Nash joined his

brother Abner in operating a mill on the Eno. And Francis Nash, in addition to practicing law and dealing in real estate, was for a time partner in a mercantile business there.

He held many public offices, and was apparently active in the Episcopal church, which was then next door to the site of the home he built on Tryon Street. He "took a leading part in the social, industrial and political life" of Hillsborough, a center of power in North Carolina.

Nash was, according to one historian, "perhaps the most attractive character of Colonial and Revolutionary Hillsborough," and that was a time when lawyers and educators and state leaders flocked to that town.

The exact date of his marriage (in 1770) is not known, but it is known that one of his two children, Ann, died as a child, and the other daughter, Sarah, grew up to marry John Waddell, a wealthy rice planter on the lower Cape Fear River. (A century later, their grandson, James Iredell Waddell, commanded the Confederate ship *Shenandoah*, the last unit of the Confederacy to fly the Confederate flag.)

Nash had married Sarah Moore in the midst of the trouble with the Regulators, and less than a year after that uprising was settled he bought the land where his house stands today. On March 21, 1772, Orange County records show, Nash bought a row of lots that totaled eight acres and covered a gentle slope rising above historic Tryon Street.

That same year he built the tall, two-story white frame house that rises above a sturdy brick basement and includes ten rooms, each with its own fireplace. The handsome floors—all original and in excellent condition today—are level and without a squeak. The graceful proportions of windows and rooms make it a home of dignity and charm.

The richly landscaped grounds, covering three acres today, include rare old trees and flowers, lovingly cared for by the present owners, Mr. and Mrs. Cecil Sanford, Jr.

It was in that home that Nash was living when he plunged

into the action that helped lead the nation into the Revolutionary War. He was a member of the second and third Provincial congresses, which met in April and August, 1775, to express opposition to British oppression.

The August meeting was held at the old St. Matthew's Episcopal Church, just down the street from Nash's home. And at that meeting, which included some of the great men in colonial history, Francis Nash was elected lieutenant colonel in the North Carolina Regiment of the Continental Army.

And Nash knew that, taking that stand, he was considered a traitor by the British. Moreover, he had troubles in his private life. Court records show that he had two illegitimate children, one of them by Ruthie Jackson, daughter of Philip Jackson, "the gentlemanly keeper of Faddis Tavern, where Ruthie was a bar maid."

Faddis Tavern, famed colonial hotel across the street from the courthouse, was the place that Lord Cornwallis stayed part of the time he was in Hillsborough. When pretty Ruthie Jackson bore Nash's daughter, he provided generously for them, deeding to Ruthie a plantation called Witty's Place, west of Hillsborough, and several slaves for the care of the place.

Records of the other illegitimate child are missing.

By February, 1776, Nash and his men were kept on the move up and down the Atlantic coast, trying to meet the changing strategy of British forces under Cornwallis.

After wearying marches through tropic bogs and winter snows, Nash and his men were back near St. Augustine, Florida, on February 5, 1777, when Nash was promoted to brigadier general.

He was popular with the men under his command, and highly valued by Gen. George Washington. The latter ordered them north again in the spring of 1777 to help beat the British back in New Jersey.

Such was the reputation of Nash and his North Carolina fighters that their march northward through Virginia and Maryland, on their way to Philadelphia, was a triumph.

During part of June and July, 1777, Nash and his men had a brief rest at Philadelphia, and Gov. Thomas Burke of North Carolina (then a member of Congress) wrote on July 5 that "Gen. Nash lodges in the same house with me."

By July 25, 1777, Nash was back with the army at Trenton, New Jersey, conferring with George Washington. He was full of confidence about the outcome of the coming showdown with the British, but worried about not hearing from home.

"My Dear Sally," he began one of his few surviving letters on July 25, 1777, "I have almost lost all hopes of hearing from you. Consider, my Dear Sally, the anxiety I must feel when I have now been [illegible] months absent from you without even hearing whether you are alive. Surely some strange fatality has [attended?] your Letters . . ."

After discussing the growing force of American troops, Nash continued: "No, my Dear Sally, I now feel the fullest assurance that can be founded on human events that nothing less than the immediate interposition of Providence (which I will not suppose can be exerted in favor of tyranny & oppression) can prevent us from the valuable blessings of Liberty, Freedom, and Independence . . .

"And with those assurances I rest satisfied with the blessing of Heaven of returning to you ere long, crowned with Victory, to spend in peace & domestick happiness, the remainder of a Life, which without you, would not be worth possessing."

Nash said that his own forces had been "re-enforced since I came here by one regiment of Virginians and an artillery corps with six brass field pieces, making the strength of my brigade, in the whole, about 2,000."

That meant, he said, that there were about 20,000 continental troops in the field, in addition to some 4,000 or 5,000 in Canada.

"Is it possible that with such an army and a *Washington* at their head that Americans can have anything to fear?" he wrote.

On the very next morning, July 26, 1777, he received orders from General Washington to march his brigade to Philadelphia that day.

"Our whole Army are on their march this Day," he added in a hurried postscript.

They were defeated by Cornwallis at Brandywine in September, and in less than a month Washington had devised a maneuver to cut off the British at Germantown, Pennsylvania. But a heavy fog lay close to the ground that dawn of October 4, 1777, and, when the shooting began, the smoke of battle made it impossible for men to see more than a few feet around them.

In that thick haze, the Americans were mistaken by some of their comrades for the enemy, and they began to retreat. But Nash was riding down the main street of Germantown, leading his men to battle, when a cannonball struck a metal sign beside the road, bounced off, and struck with such force that it killed both his horse and his aide, Major Witherspoon. It knocked Nash to the ground with a shattered thigh and horrible head wounds.

The head wounds soon blinded Nash, but he tried to conceal the thigh wound with his hand as he urged his men on toward battle.

"Never mind me," he told them, "I had a devil of a tumble. Rush on, my boys. Rush on the enemy. I'll be after you presently."

When Washington was notified of Nash's injury, he sent his personal physician to care for him, and Nash was removed to a nearby house for nursing care.

But there was no stopping the bleeding, and through three days the thirty-five-year-old Nash "lingered in extreme torture" before he died on October 7, 1777. He was such a soldier, one historian said, that he was "admired by his enemies—admired by and lamented by his companions in arms."

There was some irony, fellow officers recalled, in the fact that Nash, long admired as "the handsomest man on horseback," should have had his strong legs shattered. As one of his fellow soldiers told the story, Nash "had the finest leg that was ever hung on a man."

But they praised him equally for his "intellectual attributes, for he was one of the most enlightened, liberal, generous and magnanimous gentlemen that ever sacrificed his life for his country."

Officers gathered around his bed in his last hours said Nash's last words were: "From the first dawn of the Revolution, I have ever been on the side of liberty and my country."

General Washington was so distressed at Nash's death that he issued orders on Thursday morning, October 9, 1777, that all officers who could should attend the 10 A.M. services, near the roadside where Nash fell.

He would be buried with full military honors, with much of his army present, "at the place where the road where the troops marched on yesterday comes into the great road."

Nash was buried in a Mennonite graveyard nearby, in Kulpsville, Pennsylvania, about fifteen miles from Philadelphia.

But Nash's wife, Sally, knew nothing of his death until she looked out her front door one day and saw his body servant, Harry, who had attended the general and his two horses throughout the war. Harry was leading Nash's prized horse up the driveway, and at the sight of that riderless horse Sally knew her husband must be dead.

Less than a month after Nash's death, the Continental Congress directed that a monument be erected in his memory. Philadelphians erected a monument at his grave in 1844, and at last, in 1903, Congress built a marble arch in his memory at the Guilford Battle Ground in North Carolina. But that archway was destroyed in 1937 to make way for a widened road, and no other marker to Nash stood until the plaque was unveiled at West Point in 1977.

Within a few years after Nash's death, his widow married the officer who succeeded him, Thomas Clark. The Clarks had no children, but Francis Nash's sole heir, his daughter Sarah, was later given a 12,000-acre land grant in what is now the Cumberland Furnace area of Dickson County, in recognition of Nash's services in the Revolutionary War.

Nash had no heirs named Nash, but his brother Abner had many descendants, including the poet Ogden Nash. One of Abner's sons, Frederick Nash, was a supreme court justice in North Carolina. It was Frederick, born in the governor's palace at New Bern while his father was governor, who built the most elegant home in Hillsborough.

That house, standing on a quiet residential street just back of the Francis Nash home, was in recent years owned by Chancellor Alexander Heard of Vanderbilt University. At the University of North Carolina Heard was a classmate of Cecil Sanford, Jr., who owns the Francis Nash home.

Sanford, who is a brother of former governor Terry Sanford of North Carolina (now president of Duke University), has retired from a long career in the foreign service. He and Mrs. Sanford have furnished the house in handsome antiques and brightened it with treasures they collected in many lands.

In the years between Francis Nash and Cecil Sanford, there have been many owners of the sturdy house, including two outstanding men in the state's history. One of them, William Hooper, who bought the house in 1782, signed the Declaration of Independence. He lived there until his death on October 14, 1790, and he was buried in his garden—now part of the Old Town Cemetery that lies between the Nash house and the Presbyterian Church.

Third owner to bring fame to the house was Gov. William A. Graham, one of the most distinguished governors in North Carolina history. Graham lived there during the Civil War and his family owned the place until 1906.

Sanford, who takes great pleasure in doing the work himself, has restored the house and grounds to prime condition, and has already served for two terms as president of the thriving Hillsborough Historical Society. He is full of stories of the Hillsborough of 200 years ago, where Nash was such a dashing figure.

The fact that Richard Henderson chose to name Fort Nashborough for him in 1780, just three years after Nash's death, is not surprising. Nor is the fact that the North Carolina legislature in 1784 voted to found a town here and name it Nashville in his honor.

Gen. Francis Nash was, after all, the soldier who had won their heart above all North Carolinians, and at Nash's death Gov. R. Caswell said he considered the loss "irreparable."

"His career was a brief, but a brilliant one," one historian wrote. "It is unquestionably true that there was no officer of the American Revolution who acquired in the same period a more solid reputation for soldierly qualities, or who died more universally regretted than he."

Gen. William Lee Davidson, "Completely Adored"

From his high-spirited youth when he coaxed young men to fight for freedom to the winter night he lay naked and dead on a misty battlefield, William Lee Davidson—for whom Davidson County was named—had an unfailing magnetism.

Determined to see this country freed of British rule, he was so persuasive, so concerned for the welfare of soldiers who fought beside him, that farmers laid aside their plows and followed him to battle in the Revolutionary War.

"There was no more completely adored soldier in North Carolina," Chalmers G. Davidson wrote in the biography *Piedmont Partisan, The Life and Times of General William Lee Davidson.* "Davidson was the most popular man in the region."

February 1, 1981, marked 200 years since the sometimes reckless Davidson was killed by one of Lord Cornwallis's soldiers in a skirmish only a few miles from Davidson's home. But two centuries after his death there are still strong reminders of Davidson's hold on the affections of North Carolina.

Not only is a Tennessee county named for him, but another county, in North Carolina, also took his name. And if one journeys to Davidson College (named for him) in the town of Davidson, North Carolina (named for the college), Davidson's spirit seems to walk the peaceful campus and the charming countryside of gentle hills and quiet streams where he once rode.

Just to track down his home territory, near Charlotte, North Carolina, today is to step back more than half a century before Tennessee was founded and to feel the burden of British injustice throughout the Carolinas.

And there is no way of separating Davidson's zeal for freedom from the little Presbyterian churches that still dot the countryside of Rowan and Mecklenburg counties. Each church was center of its community, and the Scotch-Irish settlers who came there in great numbers in the 1740s had no thought of buckling under to British tyranny again. When preachers told them that freedom was their divine right, Davidson and the rest of the congregation believed.

It was in Charlotte, in fact, and in the countryside around it—in both Mecklenburg and Rowan counties—that the British found the most hostile people in the nation, according to the British general, Lord Cornwallis.

Long before the Revolutionary War began, North Carolinians were busy drawing up their own Declaration of Independence. Some twenty years before New Englanders fought at Lexington and Concord, Massachusetts, North Carolina was stirred to independence.

Davidson was born in 1746 in Lancaster County, Pennsylvania, where his Scotch-Irish father, George Davidson, and his family had settled in 1740 or 1741 after leaving their home in Derry, in North Ireland. William Lee Davidson (he added the middle name later), youngest of George's three sons, was about two years old when the family took the long wagon trail south to the wilderness of North Carolina.

George soon acquired a large farm, for a time ran a tavern where other settlers stopped on their journey south, and became a citizen of standing in the community. The exact site of his home is not known, but it is believed to have been on Davidsons Creek, named by or for his Uncle John as early as the 1740s.

Life in their neighborhood revolved around the Presbyterian church across the creek, Centre Church. In that congregation, William Lee Davidson developed the ideals that propelled him into a heroic role in the Revolutionary War, Chalmers Davidson (retired historian at Davidson College) has written.

It was a land lush with forests and tall grass, a land that eventually supported impressive plantation homes and families of solid values. George Davidson died before he built any mansion, and left William Lee Davidson fatherless at thirteen. But William was sent to a boys' academy near Charlotte, twenty miles away, and there he acquired a fair education.

According to Chalmers Davidson, William Davidson studied at Sugaw Creek Academy, operated in connection with Sugaw Creek Presbyterian Church. That church (in a later building) still stands on the same spot, near the edge of Charlotte. And in its churchyard today is buried the controversial Presbyterian minister Alexander Craighead, who shouted freedom from pulpits all over that area.

He fiercely opposed Britain's discrimination against Presbyterian churches in the colonies, and his rallying call against the British won him recognition as "Father of Independence" in the piedmont section of the Carolinas.

To young William Davidson, who as a student at Sugaw Creek Academy probably got an extra dose of Craighead's passion for independence, it must have seemed a natural sequence of events that the first "Declaration of Independence" was written in Charlotte. That Mecklenburg Declaration, written in May, 1776, and sent directly to the Founding Fathers meeting in Philadelphia, sprang from Craighead's territory.

But before the Revolutionary War came, and before William Davidson was grown, he knew the need for every farm to defend itself from Indians. As a child, he liked to "play soldier," and he was intrigued by the militia's frequent musters, where sharpshooting farmers displayed their marksmanship and their horsemanship.

Before the war came, and before Davidson married, he made his home for a time at the frame house of his cousin, George Davidson, some six or seven miles from the present Davidson College campus. And that two-story house—perhaps the oldest house standing in the area today—is particularly evocative of pioneer dignity and sturdiness.

Built perhaps in the 1760s, the house is deceptively simple on the outside. Standing on a slight rise above a narrow country road, it is being carefully restored today by a young couple of the area.

The interior of the house is full of surprises—from the original wide flooring and the corner fireplaces to the hand-carved mantel and paneling in an impressive upstairs room that measures eighteen by twenty-four feet.

It was perhaps from that room that twenty-one-year-old William Davidson and his cousin George set out in 1767 on William's first official assignment—to escort the colonial governor, the extravagant William Tryon, into Cherokee territory on a boundary-setting mission. To have been selected for the expedition was some measure of Davidson's standing in the community.

Before the year was out, Davidson's engagement to Mary Brevard, daughter of one of the leading families of the area, was announced. That was on December 10, 1767, and the marriage followed promptly.

The home that Davidson and his bride built, across Davidson Creek from Centre Church, vanished long ago, and the site is buried under the water of a lake. There seven children were born to the couple, and there, in 1770—three years after Davidson's marriage—his public career began. He was appointed constable, and that put him in charge of census taking.

Already well known in the county, Davidson was, by his reputation for fair dealing and tact, particularly fitted to enter every home and win the confidence of tax-burdened farmers. Moreover, his reputation for impartiality was a tremendous aid in keeping the peace—another of his duties as constable.

In 1772, he was commissioned captain in the Rowan County militia, taking the oath of allegiance to King George III, as the law required. At the same time, Griffith Rutherford, for whom Rutherford County, Tennessee, is named, was commissioned colonel in the same regiment. Throughout the Revolution, the military careers of the two men brought them in close contact.

In 1772 North Carolinians were chafing under the strain of heavy taxes and ruthless public officials who represented the king. Yet when a group of the rebels called Regulators fought the British in the Battle of the Alamance in 1771, the Rowan County militia took no part.

But it was a different story by August 24, 1774, when North Carolinians held their first Provincial Congress in their capital city, New Bern. Rowan County citizens, with their county seat at Salisbury, stood solidly against the extravagance of the king's officers—at the citizens' expense.

The next month, on September 23, 1774, Rowan County followed the New Bern congress with a meeting of its own, and Davidson was among the twenty-five appointed to a committee to see that the resolution of the "Continental and Provincial Congress be carried into Execution by the inhabitants of this county."

And Davidson was equally active in organizing neighboring Mecklenburg County, where he had real estate interests and long associations. Mecklenburg citizens were so outraged at the royal government that they considered changing the name of the county seat, Charlotte, which had been named for the queen.

The Mecklenburg Committee of Safety was organized in May, 1775, as the beginning of an independent government, and Davidson's brother-in-law and other family connections were among the founders.

Davidson himself gave the Mecklenburg Declaration his strong backing, and the area was stirred by news of the battles at Lexington and Concord. On August 1, 1775, the Committee of Safety met and ordered that 1,000 volunteers be "immediately embodied" and "ready at the shortest Notice to march out in Action."

At the same time, gathering ammunition was a pressing need, and Davidson was ordered to "take into his custody the powder, lead and flints in the possession of John Work and dispose of the same according to the order of the Committee."

There were always men suspected of profiteering from the war effort, and playing a two-faced game with the enemy. Davidson was appointed to investigate suspected citizens.

But the great effort throughout the war was to get able-bodied young men to serve in the army, and that campaign began in August and September, 1775. That initial drive brought hundreds to the cause.

North Carolina was to send two armies to fight the king: one in the militia, for short stretches of duty, and one in the regular Continental Army, serving under George Washington. Davidson, at different times during the war, served in both and recruited hundreds of men for both.

The militia and minutemen were controlled by North Carolina, and Davidson, at the beginning of the war, served as captain of a company of minutemen. Typically, he was the first to round up a company of 1,000 volunteers.

By April, 1776, the Continental Congress organized the Continental Army for North Carolina, and the commanding officer of one of the six new regiments was Col. Francis Nash, the man whose heroism in the Revolutionary War resulted, among other things, in Nashville's being named for him.

A week later, when Rutherford was commissioned brigadier general and given command of the militia from Salisbury, thirty-year-old Davidson was commissioned a major in the Continental Army.

After a number of skirmishes and expeditions along the Carolina coast, Davidson was ordered to march his men northward from Charleston, South Carolina, to join General Washington. But before they reached Wilmington, North Carolina, their commanding general, James Moore, died, and Gen. Francis Nash succeeded him in command.

By June, 1777, Davidson was back in home territory, recruiting men for three new regiments. Farmers often felt that protecting their families and planting their crops was as important as fighting, and deserters who had suffered through hunger, illness, and crippling wounds were determined not to offer their lives again. Yet they flocked to Davidson's side and followed him to battle.

But the army did not accept anybody who came along. No imported servants were enlisted, and recruiting officers looked for men of "moral character . . . as much as possible." The recruits were to be "able-bodied men, fit for service, capable of marching well, and such whose attachment to American liberties they have no cause to suspect; young, hearty, robust men, whose birth, family, connections and property bind them to the interest of their Country, and those well practiced in the use of fire arms. . . ."

No matter where he found them, Davidson signed up recruits that the British army under Cornwallis called "the best marksmen of the world." Most of them were good horsemen too, and Davidson, from his boyhood, had loved horses and fine horsemanship.

But lack of money to pay the soldiers, lack of food and ammunition made it difficult to hold an army together, and Davidson's men lost heart when they joined Washington's forces just as the latter retreated in defeat from the battle at Brandywine in September, 1777.

Washington retaliated with a new offensive at Germantown, Pennsylvania, on October 4, 1777, and it was in the blinding fog and confusion of that battle that General Nash was fatally wounded.

But the agony was just beginning for Davidson and his men. After the rout at Germantown, Washington marched his army to Camp Whitemarsh, fourteen miles from Philadelphia, on October 29, 1777. And by December 19, Washington was settling his army down for the winter in a strategic valley called Valley Forge, twenty-one miles from Philadelphia.

What he could not know then was that a harsh winter would trap his suffering men—"an army without tents," many of the men without clothes, without food, without pay, and often desperately ill.

No towns nearby could offer shelter, and Washington had to put the soldiers to work in deep snow to fell trees and build log barracks. Some of the men, literally without clothing or blankets, survived by huddling before fires, exposing first one side and then the other to the warmth.

The bond between Davidson and the officers and men who suffered alongside him deepened with the years. Those who survived the frozen bleakness were entitled to a furlough in the spring, Davidson thought, and in March 1778 he marched the worn and tattered army back to North Carolina.

There, after a three-month rest, Davidson began his recruiting campaign all over again, and by this time he had won the admiration of top officers in Washington's army— all veterans of the gruesome winter in Valley Forge.

One of those fellow officers, the gallant "Light-Horse Harry" Lee—Washington's great favorite and father of Gen. Robert E. Lee—so admired the tall, unswerving Davidson that he wrote a brief biography of him, describing him as "a man of popular manners, pleasing address, active and indefatigable."

In November, 1778, Davidson marched his newly recruited army north again, and Washington soon had them at work helping build fortifications at West Point. In December, 1778, Washington ordered Davidson and his men to Philadelphia to report to Benedict Arnold. Arnold's high living and extravagance were an outrage to starving soldiers and thrifty citizens there, and soon there was talk of a court-martial for Arnold.

Meantime Davidson was summoned to preside at another court-martial in Philadelphia on April 2, 1779. And that was one of many military courts that he presided over with his usual fair-mindedness. After a long furlough at home in the spring of 1780, Davidson was foiled by a British blockade when he attempted to rejoin his regiment in Charleston, South Carolina. Thus, it turned out, he escaped being taken prisoner there.

On May 29, 1780, a British massacre of Americans at the tiny Waxhaw settlement—the same massacre where thirteen-year-old Andrew Jackson learned to despise the conquering British—brought quick action by the North Carolina militia under Rutherford, with Davidson second in command.

The showdown came, for Davidson, on July 21, 1780, when he and his 200 men tried to stop a British detachment. Davidson, plunging ahead of his men, was shot through the stomach. Miraculously, after a summer of care at his home, he recovered. He was ready to fight again by September.

On August 31, 1780, he became brigadier general, and

was responsible for the men who stirred the nation with their victory at King's Mountain on October 7, 1780. He had been first choice of the men to lead them in that battle, but other duties held him elsewhere. No one could have been more jubilant than Davidson when he reported the victory at King's Mountain to the "President of Congress."

In the fall of 1780, Cornwallis began withdrawing from painfully hostile Charlotte, and Davidson hoped to strike the British a telling blow then. But a reorganization of the American forces in the Carolinas, under Gen. Nathanael Greene, delayed that maneuver.

It was not until January 31, 1781, that Davidson and two other generals sat on a log on the muddy banks of the Catawba River, pondering their strategy for keeping Cornwallis from crossing the river on his way to Salisbury, to join his main forces.

The American generals, including Greene, Morgan, and Davidson, knew that Cornwallis was just four miles away, on the other side of the rain-deepened river. They were convinced that Cornwallis would try to ford it that night—before the downpour made a crossing impossible. The question was: which of the several fords—shallow places in the river—would Cornwallis choose for his crossing?

The decision was that Greene and Morgan would withdraw their men from the area and make an all-out effort against the British later. They would leave it to Davidson to scatter his thin line of some 800 men along the river bank to patrol it. In addition, he would place 250 men at each of the two most likely crossings, to harass the British wherever they chose to ford the river.

With winter darkness falling early, there was little time after the three generals' 2 P.M. conference on a log for Davidson's men to survey their posts. But they knew there were two fords at Cowan—one where horses could cross and one where wagons could make it. Davidson placed guards at both.

To protect his men from possible attack from the rear, Davidson placed a detachment with him on a hillside about a half mile from the ford where he believed Cornwallis would cross. Davidson was to rush to the site of the battle the moment the guards gave the alarm.

Meantime, at 1 A.M. on February 1, 1781, Cornwallis marched his army through the rainy darkness and deep mud along the opposite bank, and by dawn they had reached Cowan's Ford. Cornwallis ordered his men to plunge into the waist-high, churning river and head for the opposite shore. They were not to fire at the Americans until they reached the opposite bank. Indeed they could not fire, with their guns and ammunition strapped on their backs.

Lord Cornwallis "dashed first into the river, mounted on a very fine spirited horse," and the whole British force was guided through the unfamiliar territory by a local sympathizer with the British.

One sixteen-year-old recruit in Davidson's army was among the men assigned to guard the ford, and he admitted later that he and the other guards—chilled to the bone and huddled around fires—had fallen asleep. At dawn they were awakened by the splash of Cornwallis's men and horses in the rock-bottomed river.

"The British! The British!" the terrified young guards shouted as they began firing at the Redcoats in the water.

Before they could believe it, Davidson appeared at the riverbank, surveying the scene. At that same moment, the first British soldier to rise from the river fired the first shot from their side, and it struck Davidson in the breast.

"For a moment Davidson stared in the direction of the man with the smoking gun," Chalmers Davidson wrote. "Then, without a sound, he fell from his horse," dead before his body reached the ground. And a strange silence fell on both sides of the battle.

Gen. William Lee Davidson, "Winner of Men"

On the gray, rainy dawn of February 1, 1781—the last morning of Gen. William Lee Davidson's life—an awesome silence fell on both British and American troops as the North Carolina hero fell dead.

The first bullet fired by Lord Cornwallis's troops as they climbed the bank of the swift Catawba River at Cowan's Ford had struck Davidson in the heart, and the man for whom Davidson County, Tennessee, is named died so instantly that, according to one observer, as he fell from his horse he "did not carry his life to the ground."

Davidson's green recruits fled in terror, leaving the lifeless body of their commander on the soggy ground. But the British took time to strip Davidson of all his clothes—even his billfold—and leave his naked body in the rain as they rushed on in pursuit. (His billfold is preserved today in the British Record Office in London, and a copy of its contents is at Davidson College, North Carolina, named for him.)

Officers who had served under Davidson could not stop the retreat of the young American recruits, and civilians joined them in hysterical haste—piling older members of the family, children, the sick, and all the household possessions they could manage into wagons to escape the pillaging British.

The battle of Cowan's Ford—a dismal loss for the Americans—actually resulted in the death of only three Americans in addition to Davidson, while the number of British

26

who were killed is estimated at between forty and one hundred men.

But the fact was that without Davidson his men lost their rallying point. Many of them returned to their farms and never fought again. And the fury of the British pursuit of Americans on that February 1, 1781, resulted in the burning of patriots' homes and the death of civilians.

Torrence's Tavern, about ten miles from Cowan's Ford on the road to Salisbury, had been selected as rendezvous point for American forces after the battle, but before the soldiers could get there the narrow country roads were blocked with wagonloads of civilians fleeing the British.

Indeed Cornwallis had been tipped off about the rendezvous at Torrence's Tavern, and he had sent one of his most dreaded officers, Col. Banastre Tarleton, in pursuit. In the bedlam surrounding Torrence's Tavern, confused American soldiers did little to stop the British.

"The militia formed as best they could, but their General's death had left them befuddled," Chalmers G. Davidson wrote in his biography, *Piedmont Partisan, The Life and Times of General William Lee Davidson.*

"The dock-tailed British cavalry, the nightmare of the helpless, put all to flight. Beds were ripped up and feathers covered the lane. Furniture was battered to pieces and chickens beheaded. Ten dead Americans, several of them old men and unarmed, were left on the ground by the dragoons of 'bloody Tarleton'."

Next day, the British burned down Torrence's Tavern, and burned down the home of John Brevard, outstanding citizen in the area and father-in-law of General Davidson.

Meantime, during the night of February 1, three of Davidson's friends (Maj. David Wilson, Richard Barry, and the Reverend Thomas H. McCaule) dared to brave the enemy-held territory to search for the body of Davidson on the battlefield beside Cowan's Ford.

They laid the bare body of the young general across Wilson's horse and rode to a nearby house, the home of Wilson's mother, where she found a suit of clothes that had belonged to her patriot brother, James Jack (in 1775 he had delivered the Mecklenburg Declaration of Independence to the Continental Congress in Philadelphia).

Meantime a neighbor of Davidson's, George Templeton, had broken the news of the general's death to his wife, Mary. Though her seventh child was only one month old and the enemy were all around, she rode horseback the fifteen miles through the darkness to the Wilson home to see her dead husband.

Hastily she and a small group of friends accompanied Davidson's body to the nearest church—Hopewell Presbyterian Church (one of the most imposing in the area)—and, without benefit of coffin, buried him in a midnight service by torchlight in the churchyard. There, in mist and by flickering flame, the Reverend McCaule, a close friend of Davidson, said the benediction. And Chalmers G. Davidson quotes, with few changes, a strikingly appropriate poem describing "The Burial of Sir John Moore" by Charles Wolfe:

> They buried him darkly at dead of night,
> The sods with their bayonets turning.
> By the struggling moonbeams' misty light
> And the torches dimly burning.
> No useless coffin enclosed his breast,
> Nor in sheet or in shroud they wound him;
> But he lay like a warrior taking his rest
> With his martial cloak around him.
> Few and short were the prayers they said,
> And they spoke not a word of sorrow;
> But they steadfastly gazed on the face that was dead
> And bitterly thought of the morrow.
> Slowly and sadly they laid him down,

From the field of his fame fresh and gory;
They carved not a line, they raised not a stone,
But left him alone with his glory.

To finish the war without Davidson's leadership was a struggle for North Carolina. Nobody else could stir new recruits to battle. Officers and men soon realized the wide-ranging effect of their loss. The war that they had hoped to end in a few days dragged on for eight more months.

"You may rely upon it that the fall of General Davidson has left the people without a head in whom they have confidence as an officer," Congressman William Sharpe of North Carolina wrote to General Washingon. "From my particular knowledge of that part of the country I can venture to say that we have lost more than 500 men in the common defence."

The loss of those 500 men who refused to fight without Davidson was felt by "Light-Horse Harry" Lee.

"The loss of Brigadier Davidson would have been felt in any stage of the war," Lee wrote. "It was particularly detrimental in its effect at this period, for he was the chief instrument relied upon by Greene for the assemblage of militia, an event all important at this crisis and anxiously desired by the American general."

General Greene admitted two days after Davidson's death that he had to change his strategy after the loss of Davidson. Nobody else could get recruits.

"The loss of General Davidson is a great misfortune at this time," Greene wrote to Gen. Thomas Sumter. "I stayed at one of the places of rendezvous the night after the enemy crossed until midnight, but not a man appeared, nor was there a single man joined us except a few belonging to South Carolina."

The British general, Lord Cornwallis, was jubilant in his report to the colonial secretary of state in Britain. He said that the events of February 1 had "so effectually dispirited the Militia that we met with no further opposition in our march to the Yadkin, through one of the most rebellious tracts in America."

It was odd that General Davidson, a man who had had no opportunity to command in a brilliant battle and no chance to prove the soundness of the strategy he plotted, had such a grip on the loyalty of both soldiers and civilians.

His devotion to freedom and his determination to fight for it were part of his power. His kindness to soldiers who suffered alongside him and his fairness in dealing with others—whether as county magistrate in his youth or as presiding officer in courts-martial during his military career—sealed a strong bond.

There was a warmth and enthusiasm about him that touched their hearts, and one old lady of the area wrote that sixty years after his death women mourned him. She wrote of "the thrill of agony which ran through the hearts of the people when the news flew from house to house that brave, good Richard Barry and his comrades were bringing the blood-stained corpse of General William Davidson from Cowan's Ford to the house of his aged friend, Mrs. Samuel Wilson.

"We cannot understand," she wrote, "how it was that women who were no kin to him wrung their hands and wept, and why 60 years afterward the tragic tale was told in hushed and saddened tones."

Meantime, on the night of Davidson's burial at Hopewell Presbyterian Churchyard, his wife, the former Mary Brevard, had to think of how she would bring up the seven young children that her thirty-five-year-old husband had left in her care.

In the less than fourteen years of their marriage, three daughters and four sons were born—the youngest of them, William Lee Davidson II, only a month before his father's death. It was that youngest son who did most to commemorate his heroic father.

In 1835, in the parlor of his home—still standing 2½ miles from the Davidson College campus today—outstanding Presbyterians of the area met several times "at early candle light" to plan location of Davidson College, named for the general.

William Lee Davidson II was fifty-four years old then, and his comfortable home, called Beaver Dam (built in 1829 and now the home of Chalmers G. Davidson), was center of a thriving plantation, with twenty-five or thirty slaves on it.

Davidson's land included 469 acres to the west of his home, and these he donated to the college after it was named for his father. And the church he attended, Hopewell Presbyterian, had other members who took a lead in founding the college.

Davidson was the first big contributor to the college, and served as trustee from 1836 to 1853. He had married his cousin "Betsy Lee" Davidson, daughter of Maj. John Davidson, owner of one of the grand plantations of the area. They had no children, but the many great-nieces and nephews and the members of the student body at Davidson College found some of their happiest hours at the hospitable home of "Uncle Billy Lee" and "Aunt Betsy Lee," at Beaver Dam.

When Betsy Lee Davidson died, William Lee Davidson II buried her beside his father in the most elaborate tomb in Hopewell Churchyard. Soon he moved to Marengo County, Alabama, where he became even more prosperous. His second marriage was to a widow, Mrs. Sarah Houston, and at his death he left the college "a handsome legacy."

But William Lee Davidson II, as a small boy, had lived a while in what is now Tennessee—near Nashville, in fact. It was not until 1783—two years after General Davidson's death—that North Carolina got around to paying his widow 1,033 pounds in recognition of his services during the Revolutionary War. The currency had so depreciated in value that the gift was a pittance.

In that same year, North Carolina created one huge county from its land west of the mountains (now the area included in the state of Tennessee) and named it Davidson County in honor of General Davidson.

Land grants were the usual way of rewarding soldiers or their heirs, and in 1785 North Carolina gave 5,750 acres of land to General Davidson's heirs. That land lay in what is now Stewart County.

The general's widow chose not to live in that far western part of the county, but near the little settlement of Nashville, on a 200-acre farm in what is now East Nashville. There she would be near the outstanding academy at Spring Hill, established by the Presbyterian minister, the Reverend Thomas Craighead.

The farm where General Davidson's widow and children lived near Nashville was "on the north side of Cumberland River, below the mouth of Dry Creek, one mile below the mouth and near the Buffalo Crossing"—not far from the later site of Edgefield Junction.

There the Davidsons lived until most of the children were married. Two of the children moved to Mississippi after their marriages, and two moved to Kentucky. One moved to Missouri, and two returned to North Carolina.

There were many intermarriages between the Davidsons and the Brevards, and between the Davidsons and the Ewings and the children of Ephraim McLean, trustee and treasurer of Nashville's Davidson College (established in 1785 and named for General Davidson, it was a forerunner of the present Peabody College).

Margaret ("Peggy") Davidson, fourth child of General

Davidson, married the distinguished Finis Ewing, one of the founders of the Cumberland Presbyterian Church. Peggy, "distinguished for beauty of person, strength of character and amiability," was a strong backer of her husband in his long struggle for leadership within the church —his chief opponent being the Reverend Thomas Craighead, son of the Reverend Alexander Craighead, the great leader to Revolution in their home county in North Carolina.

The descendants of Peggy Davidson and Finis Ewing are the most prominent of General Davidson's descendants. Their son, William Lee Davidson Ewing, became governor of Illinois and a U.S. senator from that state. His brother, Ephraim Brevard Ewing, became secretary of state of Missouri.

One son of General Davidson, George Lee, was active in early Tennessee government, and when he returned to North Carolina to live he was elected for nine consecutive sessions to that state's House of Commons.

A granddaughter of General Davidson, Anna Ewing, married Francis M. Cockrell, a brigadier general in the Confederate army and a United States senator from Missouri for many years.

In 1795, fourteen years after General Davidson's death, his widow remarried and returned to North Carolina. Her second husband, Robert Harris, had lost one hand in the Revolutionary War and was a prominent citizen of Cabarrus County, North Carolina. She survived him by many years, lived to be about ninety, and is said to have died in the home of one of her daughters in Logan County, Kentucky.

For 139 years after his death, there was no tombstone at General Davidson's grave, apparently because his widow and children thought the government was going to erect one. For just eight months after Davidson's death in 1781,

Congress had passed a resolution to erect a monument in his memory. His family must have assumed that the monument would be at his grave.

But Congress soon forgot its resolution, and it was not until 1920 that North Carolina patriots had a monument placed at his grave, near the entrance of the stately old brick church still active as Hopewell Presbyterian Church. There, where tall trees are reflected in the high arched windows, on a hill looking down on a peaceful churchyard enclosed by a stone wall, the Davidson marker stands today.

Congress did not get around to erecting its long-promised monument until 1906—125 years after Davidson's death. That monument, at Guilford Court House battleground, was torn down in 1937, condemned as a "traffic hazard."

Meantime North Carolina, after the original Davidson County broke away from the state and became Tennessee, created another Davidson County of its own in 1822, and that county was cut off from Rowan County, the general's old home territory.

Thus today he is remembered by Davidson County, Tennessee, by another county of the same name in North Carolina; by Davidson College with its enrollment of 1,331 students; by the town of Davidson, North Carolina, with a population of 3,260; and by Peabody College in Nashville, which grew out of Davidson Academy.

"Never was there a more intrepid soldier, never a greater patriot, never did a man love his country with more ardent affection," early historian John Haywood wrote of Davidson. "His name should be ever dear to the people of North Carolina and Tennessee, and the posterity which he left should be dear to them also."

James Robertson, Founder of Nashville

James Robertson, the "uncommonly quiet" man who swam icy rivers to keep appointments with Indians, the Indian fighter who spent much of his life defending their rights, did more than any other man to turn Tennessee into a white man's land.

Robertson, whose name loops along the parkway back of Capitol Hill and leaps out of Tennessee history in countless directions, cut a bloody trail through the canebrake to found Nashville.

Two of his sons were beheaded by Indians and two of his brothers met death at the hands of Indians. Another of his sons—a twelve-year-old lad at the time—was scalped in a clearing of cedar trees on what is now Capitol Hill while the boy's mother, the indomitable Charlotte, watched in horror from her lookout at Fort Nashborough.

Robertson's closest friends were murdered, kidnapped, scalped by Indians. But there was no turning back for him.

Today his name lives on in Robertson County. And Charlotte's name lives on in Charlotte Avenue, Charlotte Road, and the town where it ends, called Charlotte. The little Fort Nashborough replica near the river's edge in downtown Nashville today reminds Nashvillians and tourists what life was like when Robertson and his followers lived in the original log fort very near that spot.

But no memorial today can tell the heartbreak, hunger, and raw adventure that Robertson and his men encountered on the frozen crags and sleety paths they followed to settle the present Nashville.

No Nashvillian today can walk through downtown Nashville without touching Robertson's work and his steel-cold courage. No one can drive out Harding Road without following Indian trails he staked out for a road.

No one can stroll through Centennial Park without touching the farm where Robertson's stalwart sister brought up her family—one of them, Mark Cockrill, to gain international fame as "wool king of the world."

No one can drive out Eighth Avenue, N., toward the old St. Cecelia Academy, without following the driveway to the home one of Robertson's daughters built on that same hill and called Buena Vista ("Fine View").

The treaties that closemouthed Robertson worked out with Indians, trying to establish peace and trade with them, marked him as a diplomat. His unquestioned word, his stern enforcement of terms, his determination to make the white man live up to his agreement with the Indians made him an invaluable link between the two peoples.

Robertson slept in Indian huts, ate of their sometimes sickening food, spoke their language through days of patient negotiating. In rainy forests and flooded swamps he traveled to meet Cherokee, Chickasaw, Choctaw, and Creek.

The persistence he showed in sticking by the tiny settlement at Nashville when slaughter by Indians turned scores back east helped establish the boundary of the United States at the Mississippi River (rather than at the Appalachians) at the end of the Revolutionary War. For we were still part of the British colonies when young Robertson struck out westward from his North Carolina home in 1770 to see what the Tennessee side of the mountain looked like.

At that time, Tennessee was the western end of North Carolina and Kentucky was the western end of Virginia.

And farmers in North Carolina, incensed at the injustice of excessive taxes and tyrannical tax collectors, were eager to push westward—beyond Britain's grasp.

It was 211 years ago, and twenty-eight-year-old Robertson—setting out alone on his horse, with his dog at his heels—was soon trapped in one of the severest trials of his danger-packed life.

He had successfully crossed the mountains into what is now Tennessee and discovered the poetic valley of the Watauga, near what is now Elizabethton. After he put out a corn crop, he started home again to get his wife and son.

But on his way back to North Carolina, Robertson was caught in heavy rains, day after day, and mountain streams became wild torrents flooding the countryside. Paths were covered and landmarks blotted out, and for fourteen days Robertson wandered in the wilderness, completely lost.

A lean, muscular, compact man, he sprang lightly through the forests then and leapt across mountain streams. Shooting game for food was no problem.

But in the penetrating rains his gunpowder got wet, and he could not dry it out. When he tried to take shortcuts by scaling mountain walls, he finally had to make a choice: the climbs were too steep for his horse.

In desperation, he turned the horse loose and had to make the rest of the journey home on foot. There was little time for sleep and almost nothing to eat, and the seriously weakened Robertson doubted that he could survive.

Near the end of his endurance, he finally met two hunters —both mounted. Strangely, they refused him a ride, but gave him food and directions back to civilization.

Two years before, Robertson had married Charlotte Reeves, daughter of a Presbyterian minister in Wake County, North Carolina, and they had one son—the first of thirteen children. When Robertson returned in the spring of 1770 to tell her of the rich Watauga Valley, he soon persuaded sixteen other families—a total of eighty people —to accompany them to the rich valley.

The lure of the new land—thousands of acres there almost for the taking—made it easy for men to follow. And Robertson knew how to organize an expedition—what tools to take on pack horses, what seeds and domestic animals they would need.

Dark-haired, with keen ears and steady blue eyes that could detect signs of Indians on the path at great distances, Robertson trained the party for a variety of emergencies. Four years after they were established at Watauga, he called all of the inhabitants into their log fort to make ready for a tremendous battle.

"Our scouts this moment come in," Robertson wrote to Virginia headquarters hastily on July 20, 1776, "and have discovered the tracks of about 100 Indians coming along the path, toward our fort. . . . I am sure they will attack in the morning.

"Myself and the other officers are in good spirits and will do all we can and hope to keep them out until you can assist us with more men. Farewell."

There were actually more than three hundred Indians, and Robertson had fewer than forty men to fight them off. His fame from that victory traveled far, among both Indians and white men. And the battle showed the frontier's part in international events. For both Britain and Spain, from time to time over a twenty-five-year period, paid Indian agents to harass frontier settlements so that Americans would abandon them.

But long before the first white man came to what is now Nashville, the Indians had deserted this area. A vast parkland, Middle Tennessee was used only for hunting and fishing. And, in the unending wars between the tribes, it was a battlefield.

Robertson had been induced to explore the Nashville

area by the wealthy and imaginative Richard Henderson of Hillsborough, North Carolina, who—in one of the boldest real estate ventures in history—"bought" what is now most of Kentucky and Tennessee from the Indians.

Henderson had Daniel Boone exploring Kentucky for him at the same time he had Robertson scouting the Nashville area. And Robertson, a surveyor with plans of his own for vast landholdings, headed a band of eight white men and one slave who first explored what is now Nashville in 1779. They stayed just long enough to plant corn in a clearing.

There was in fact already a clearing in the forests around the springs called French Lick (now Nashville), where thousands of buffalo, deer, bears, and wildlife of wide variety had beaten down the tall cane to drink at the springs and lick the salt.

Indians had followed the buffalo paths that connected spring to spring throughout the area, and early French traders had followed those same paths when they came to buy furs from Indian trappers. Those paths would lead pioneers into the area and, in many cases, lay the way for Nashville's main thoroughfares.

Some of the French traders had built temporary shelter near the springs (where old Sulphur Dell baseball park was later built). And when Robertson and his band of nine followers returned to Watauga with tales of land so rich it grew cane twenty feet tall, hundreds were ready to follow him to French Lick.

Robertson decided that most of the men should go first, in the fall of 1779, to build a fort and cabins for their families. They would travel by land, taking supplies on pack horses, and herding cattle.

Because of the rough terrain, Robertson decided that the women should go by boat. Some thirty men, under the command of Col. John Donelson, would escort the women and children to French Lick.

Nobody there could know that the fall and winter of 1779 would be among the coldest on record. And Robertson, in total confidence, led the 226 men and boys and their caravan out of Ft. Patrick Henry (where Kingsport is today) in November, 1779.

As they climbed windswept mountains and forded icy streams in below-zero cold, there was sleet in their hair and hunger in their stomachs. For the 400-mile trail through Kentucky—the only known path westward then—looped far to the north and then southward again through paths close to what is now Glasgow and Bowling Green, Kentucky.

Entering Tennessee through what is now Sumner County, Robertson and his shivering band first sighted Nashville from what is now the East Nashville side of Cumberland River. The river was frozen so thick that men, pack horses, and livestock walked across to climb the bluff to French Lick on Christmas Day, 1779.

Strangely, after that month-long ordeal, not a man fell ill, and no Indians bothered them on the trail. But they could hardly have imagined anything worse than the hardships suffered by the men, women, and children just setting out on their winding, 1,000-mile voyage up and down four rivers to reach French Lick four months later.

There were some four hundred people in the party when Donelson led them out of Ft. Patrick Henry (Kingsport) in some thirty-three flatboats, canoes, and dugouts on December 22, 1779. Donelson, on the largest boat, the *Adventure,* had thirty families on board, including Mrs. James Robertson and the five Robertson children. Donelson's own family, including his daughter Rachel (later Mrs. Andrew Jackson), were among the 160 passengers on that boat, according to Thomas Edwin Matthews in his book, *General James Robertson, Father of Tennessee.*

Some flatboats had twenty-eight persons on board, and one of them suffered a horrid fate. Smallpox broke out among the passengers and, to prevent spread of the disease, the boat dropped a short distance behind the rest of the flotilla.

But Indians along the river banks seized the isolated boat and either killed or kidnapped all passengers. The screams of "poor Stuart, his family and friends" were torture to passengers in the other boats, who were helpless in the disaster.

By then it was March, 1780, and a number of those who had begun the river trip (first on the Holston, then the Tennessee, then the Ohio, then the Cumberland) had been killed or kidnapped by Indians. Boats had been sunk, had snagged on rocks, had been tossed in "high seas" in wind-whipped floodwaters.

There were heroes and heroines—like the woman who bore a child one night and the next day worked mightily to help free a boat beached on rocks. There were two cowardly men who deserted the party under attack. There were women who manned the boats while bullets cut through their skirts.

Food ran low, and the fringe of Indians standing out against the sky along the bluff-tops as the flotilla passed by kept Donelson's party from stopping to hunt.

But it was not meat they needed so much as bread and vegetables. "No meat but fat bear" made poor fare, and corn at $200 a bushel (the price Henderson had to pay at one point) would have been a bargain.

At last, on a fine spring day—April 24, 1780—more than four months after they had left Kingsport, Donelson's scarred fleet rounded the bend in the river near the spot where Nashville's Public Square stands today. The joy of the reunited families was marred only by the report of those they had lost from the original 400. The site that

Robertson had chosen for the fortress, called Fort Nashborough, lay slightly north of where the replica stands today. The spot was selected to include a fine water supply,
a spring of clear water that "dashed down the precipice,
giving great charm and interest to the location."

Some historians believe the spring gushed out of the
bluff at the point where Church Street ends at the river's
edge today (Church Street was originally called Spring
Street). It is known that the original Fort Nashborough
(named in honor of Gen. Francis Nash, Henderson's friend
who was killed in the Revolutionary War) reached from the
Church Street area up the hill to the southern border of the
Public Square.

Some of the men claimed land nearby and went to work
immediately to build their own cabins and the fortifications
around them, called "stations."

On May 13, 1780, less than a month after Donelson's
party arrived, 256 men representing eight "stations" in the
area gathered at Fort Nashborough to sign the Cumberland Compact.

Henderson, who had set up a real estate office here,
wrote the compact. A lawyer, a man of influence and grand
schemes, he led the settlers in establishing rules for their
protection and government.

Suddenly Fort Nashborough was the western front in the
Revolutionary War. Both the British and the Spanish had
agents working among the Indians to harass the American
settlers.

Indians had attacked often (thirty-seven men were killed
that year) and one of the attacks came as a party from Fort
Nashborough was helping John Donelson harvest his first
corn crop, in the Clover Bottom area, on Stone's River.

Before the attack was over, two of the men, including
James Robertson's brother, John Randolph Robertson,
had been killed by Indians. During the next few months

other farmers were killed as they tried to clear their fields, and James Robertson traveled to Kentucky for more ammunition to prepare for the Indian battles shaping up.

He left his family at Freeland's Station, about a mile away from Fort Nashborough, and there another son, Felix Robertson (later to serve twice as mayor of Nashville), was born. This first white child born in Nashville became a physician and a leader in city and state medical societies.

Four days after his child was born, Robertson returned to Nashville, and that night Indians attacked Freeland's Station. Two white men were killed before the battle was won, and the Indians were still shooting from a distance the next morning when Robertson and his family—including Charlotte with the infant in her arms—rode on horseback to the safety of Fort Nashborough.

It was about a year after the *Adventure* arrived at Fort Nashborough that the Cherokees came close to trapping Robertson—and the fort—in disaster. Three of the Indians approached the fort, and twenty of Robertson's men rode out on horseback after them, early in the morning.

Robertson's men dashed down the hill, toward what is now Broad Street, and quickly dismounted so that they could have their hands free to load their guns. Suddenly there were Indians leaping out of the canebrake and underbrush on all sides, and they closed in behind the white men to cut them off from the fort.

But the sight of horses to be captured distracted the Indians, and they followed the horses on a wild chase up what is now Capitol Hill. Mrs. Robertson, watching from a porthole in the log fortress, gave the order to loose the hounds from the fort, and the whole pack—some forty or fifty hounds—took out after the red men.

Retreating before the attack of the barking dogs, the Indians gave the white men their chance to return inside the gates of Fort Nashborough, and the returning horses were close at heel. But five white men had been killed in the battle, and two were wounded.

After the battle was over (according to a descendant, Mrs. Sarah Foster Kelley, in her book *Children of Nashville*), James Robertson "took several men and the hounds" up on Capitol Hill, where Mrs. Robertson had seen Indians standing over the body of her twelve-year-old son, Jonathan.

The boy had been scalped and was unconscious, but he was still living when his father reached him. Robertson performed surgery he had been taught (boring a hole in the boy's skull to allow drainage) and Charlotte nursed Jonathan back to health.

In the increasing horror over Indian atrocities, many of the first settlers turned back to Kentucky and the Carolinas for safety. But Robertson would not budge.

"As for me and my family, we will fight it out here," Robertson announced resolutely.

He was eager to settle his 2,000 acres in the area, where he was eventually to own 33,000 acres and a number of town lots. As surveyor, he was often hired to survey land granted other settlers, and surveyors were paid one-third of the land they surveyed.

Not until 1783, when the Revolutionary War officially ended, did the momentum of Indian attacks begin to slow down, and that year Robertson began work on a two-story brick mansion on his 2,000-acre farm in the bend of the Cumberland River (including the area where the state prison and prison farm are now). He called that home Travelers' Rest.

That same year, on June 1, Robertson called a meeting of Indian chiefs, and for three days—under a huge oak tree on what is now Charlotte Pike—they discussed peace and the trade that would profit all of them.

By 1784, the Indians had killed sixty-two of the first settlers in Nashville, and at one time not more than seventy white men were left. At that moment, the Cherokees could summon 2,000 warriors and the Creeks 5,000 in the area.

But Robertson, as a representative in the North Carolina legislature, pushed legislation through to grant 640 acres of land to settlers who stayed in Nashville and to heirs of those killed in the effort.

He pushed through incorporation of the town to be called Nashville (changed from the British form, Nashborough, out of hatred of the English and admiration of the French in the Revolution and afterward). The town was laid off in 200 lots of one acre each, and four acres were set aside for the Public Square.

It was Robertson too who pushed through legislation in North Carolina that would establish Davidson Academy (later the University of Nashville, forerunner of today's George Peabody College) in Nashville in 1785.

But the tomahawk was still the terror, and in May, 1786, Robertson's brother Mark was killed by Indians as he traveled from the home of another brother, Elijah, near the present Hermitage, to his own home (where Centennial Park is now).

That same year, Robertson's family moved into their big brick house with glass windows and six columns across the front, and shortly afterwards, in March, 1787, Robertson's twelve-year-old son, Peyton, was tapping maple trees a short distance back of the house when Charlotte heard the boy scream.

She turned the hounds loose to fight attacking Indians, but before help could arrive Peyton Robertson had been beheaded, and his young friend, John Johnston, had been kidnapped. (It was twelve years later that James Robertson found the kidnapped youth and freed him in an exchange of prisoners with the Cherokees.)

Another of the Robertson sons, Jonathan, narrowly missed death again when a bullet pierced the brim of his hat. And James Robertson was shot through the foot as he worked in his fields.

Then in December, 1793, another son, James Randolph Robertson, was trapping beaver with a friend on Caney Fork River. Both were twenty-one years old, but James Robertson worried when the young men were gone longer than they had planned.

A traveler from East Tennessee brought the awful news: both young men had been killed by the Cherokees. Young Robertson had been beheaded and his head placed on a pole and paraded in triumph around a Cherokee town.

The special victory for them was that their victim was the son of Brig. Gen. James Robertson, who had been commissioned commandant of the militia by President George Washington.

It is no wonder that, when word came that the Creeks and the Cherokees were about to invade the Cumberland settlement in 1794, Robertson organized an expedition of 550 mounted infantry to head the Indians off in their own villages.

In that Nickajack Expedition, when Robertson's men routed the Indians from their villages on September 13, 1794, the white men found inside the red men's homes the scalps of white people killed in the Nashville area. They found women who had been kidnapped and worked as slaves in the Indians' fields.

Some fifty Indians were killed in the Nickajack battle, and after that the Indians were eager to set peace talks. By November 7 and 8, 1794, they were passing the peace pipe around to Robertson.

By the time Tennessee became a state, on June 1, 1796, the worst of the Indian fighting was over. Life was coming out of the log cabins and into brick mansions. Hundreds of newcomers were moving in, some of them with pianos and harps for their parlors and fine china for their tables.

Robertson's younger children were sent away to school in the East—Felix to study medicine at the University of Pennsylvania and Lavinia to attend finishing school in Philadelphia.

James Robertson had founded the highly prosperous ironworks at Cumberland Furnace, in what is now Dickson County. His sons and daughters married into some of the most influential families in Tennessee and left their imprint on architecture, church, school, and social life of the area. And Robertson, in his later years, tackled still another frontier problem—an odd one for an old Indian fighter. As commissioner of Indian affairs, working for the U.S. government among the Chickasaws near Memphis, he used all of his diplomatic skill to guarantee fair treatment for the Indians.

In 1805, when he was sixty-three years old, Robertson thought nothing of making an 800-mile trip on horseback, through the swamps, in sweltering heat, to confer with the Indians. When it was too hot to travel by day, he traveled by moonlight. And he knew by experience to take his own cook and food with him.

Carefully observing the protocol of the tribe, he entertained at dinner almost daily, inviting as many as twenty-nine chiefs at a time to sit around his table in the cabin assigned him. His feasts of meat and bread, along with delicacies seasoned with nutmeg and cinnamon, included anchovies, pickles, wine, and brandy.

When the War Department complained about the expense account, Robertson's fellow commissioner, Silas Dinsmoor, reported that "an Indian can eat enough at one meal to last him a week." Dinsmoor added that there was "a score of these Falstaffs in the woods."

Not only land agreements, but also valuable assistance during the War of 1812 came from the Indians who respected Robertson. Friends he had made among the Choctaws and Chickasaws helped prevent further trouble from the Creeks.

In 1813, Robertson was furious about "villainous white people robbing, plundering and stealing from the Chickasaws." He interceded on behalf of the Indians in every injustice, demanding that our government pay for their losses.

In December, 1813, when Robertson was seventy-two years old, he was caught in torrential rains as he rode on horseback to keep an appointment with Choctaws near Memphis. In that cold rain, he did not hesitate to swim the swollen creeks.

"As there have been excessive rains—indeed all the creeks have been swimming for weeks—I had to swim all the creeks," Robertson wrote on December 9, 1813.

The next April, he had hurried back to Nashville to attend to a lawsuit in court when he suffered an attack of rheumatism that kept him in bed for two weeks.

But he was impatient to return to his work among the Chickasaws, and, in great pain, he returned there on horseback. He was still working among the Indians that summer when he wrote his wife, Charlotte, asking her to come down from Nashville and bring a feather bed.

There, in the Chickasaw town near Memphis, he died on September 1, 1814. And there he was buried until his son, Dr. Felix Robertson, had the body brought back to Nashville in 1825 for burial at the old City Cemetery, which he had designed.

In this cemetery Robertson and Charlotte, who outlived him by thirty years and died at age ninety-two, are buried —practically in the center of the city they both fought for and suffered for so mightily nearly two hundred years ago.

Indian Fighter John Rains
in "This Perilous Wilderness"

Not all of the tinseled excitement of the annual state fair can match the real-life adventures of wily, sharp-eyed John Rains, the famed Indian fighter who was the first white man to own the land where the fairgrounds are today.

For fifty years, steel-nerved Rains lived on that land, and if visitors to the fair today could pull aside the curtain and glance back through two-hundred years, they might spy Rains crouching in the underbrush, his ears cocked for any clue to the "red rascals," as he called all Indians.

For the 103 acres in the fairgrounds today are less than one-sixth of the 640-acre farm that Rains had surveyed in 1784. It was granted by the state of North Carolina in 1786 at a cost of ten pounds (British money) per 100 acres.

And the fort he built to protect his family stood on a hill near what is now the intersection of Rains Avenue and Merritt Avenue, high above Fourth Avenue, S. Rains built his fort to include his hilltop home and to run down the bluff to include the springs that were the family water supply, "so that we could go to it at all times in safety," his son John wrote years later. "The alarms from the Indians were almost constant."

That spring still flows today in rainy season, and it bubbles out of a weedy hillside behind a parking lot just east of Jim Coursey's Barbecue Pit at 1405 Fourth Avenue, S. And the mile-wide sweep of land that Rains owned, straddling "the big road to Nashville" (now Nolensville Road) and running along both sides of Brown's Creek, includes some of the most spectacular hilltop views in Nashville. But protecting that land—fairgrounds and all—from the Indians was a bloodcurdling affair in the 1780s and 1790s. Men, women, and children in the Nashville area were scalped, sometimes mutilated and beheaded, and sometimes kidnapped to work as slaves for the Indians.

For the Indians were determined to run the white man out of the Nashville area when Rains and his family arrived here on Christmas Day, 1779, to cross the frozen Cumberland on foot in that coldest winter on record. The ice was so thick that even the horses and cattle crossed on foot, and John Rains—the only man to bring livestock on that hazardous journey—herded seventeen horses and twenty-one cattle.

Rains, with that caravan of valuable livestock, was obviously a man of substance. In a day when a horse was not only transportation but also chief aid in getting farm work done, Rains was, in a sense, the best-equipped man among the settlers who came with James Robertson to establish Fort Nashborough. And Rains has gone down in history as "the first man to introduce neat cattle and horses upon the west side of the Cumberland River and into Middle Tennessee."

A native of Culpeper, Virginia, he was escorting his family with a group of Virginians to Harrodsburg, Kentucky, when they met James Robertson and his party on their way to what is now Nashville, in the fall of 1779.

Robertson persuaded Rains to give up his Kentucky plans and join the party on its way to French Lick (now Nashville), but it was no easy decision. As Rains said later, deciding between Kentucky and Tennessee was "like the man who wanted a wife, and knew of two beautiful women, either of whom would suit, and he wanted them both."

It turned out that Capt. John Rains was the best Indian

scout Robertson had in his Cumberland settlement, and over and over he sent Rains out to see how near the threatening Indians had come. When there was war with the Indians, Robertson sent Rains ahead to scout the territory and report on the number of Indians they had to face.

For it was not just his wife and many children that Rains had to defend. It was all of the Nashville settlement, including Fort Nashborough, on the river bank, between what is now Church Street and the courthouse.

Robertson, in command of Fort Nashborough, counted mightily on Rains to scent out roving bands of Indians before they could strike. Rains, who knew the various tribes by their costumes, their habits, and their methods of warfare, would ride like the wind through unmarked territory and come back with a clear picture of who would strike, and when.

He was so skilled with the gun that he could reload a heavy rifle as he ran. He was so good a shot that in one winter he killed thirty-two bears—most of them on his fairgrounds farm, along Brown's Creek, and in the nearby hills.

Rains—a happy, sometimes singing, sometimes rhyming, plain-talking man—could be forgiven in later years for swaggering a bit about outsmarting the Indians. For he had the record to prove it. He was, in fact, one of the twenty-odd "long hunters" who first crossed the mountains from North Carolina and Virginia in 1769 to scout the territory now known as Kentucky and Tennessee.

On June 2, 1769, more than ten years before the first permanent settlers arrived, Rains—along with other daring men whose names live on in places like Drake's Creek, Bledsoe's Lick, and Mansker's Creek—met for the expedition from Virginia.

Not until April of the following year did they return from the "long hunt" and thereby earn the name "The Long

Hunters." Through the tall grass of what is now Kentucky and Tennessee they had found their way, and they were amazed at the rich land and the plentiful game.

The wondrous tales they told when they returned to their Virginia and North Carolina homes—tales of buffalo herds by the thousands, of tall cane and towering forests and plentiful springs in the Cumberland Valley, a land where no Indians lived—matched the stories of Daniel Boone and his explorers.

The excitement of "moving west" swept across Virginia and North Carolina like a fever, and when Richard Henderson of Hillsborough, North Carolina, worked out terms with the Indians for purchasing their Tennessee lands on March 17, 1775, the stage was set for the great migration.

But there were Indians who hated the terms of the treaty, and a few months after the first permanent settlers arrived at Fort Nashborough, the Indians began their murderous attacks. There were Spanish and French traders who paid the Indians to kill off the white settlers. And there were, during the American Revolution, English agents who paid the Indians to harass the American frontiersmen.

Shawnees, Chickasaws, Cherokees, Choctaws, and Creeks had fought over the land for centuries and had, in fact, almost sealed their own doom by their tribal warfare. And in the years after the first white settlers came, the warring tribes shifted from one side to another—sometimes to other Indians, sometimes to the Spanish, French, English, or Americans.

By 1784, when John Rains staked out his farm that included the present fairgrounds, he had tracked Indians up and down Brown's Creek and all of the other creeks around Nashville. And he could stand at the high ridge where his fort stood (now Rains Avenue) and tell, at the sound of guns at Fort Nashborough, how desperate the need was for reinforcements. On his swift horses, with his son Billy riding beside him, he could make it to the fort in short order. But Captain Rains, when he arrived with his family at the present Nashville on Christmas Day, 1779, had no idea that the Indians would harass the area. On the very day that he arrived at Fort Nashborough, he was so sure of safe living that he rode out to select the land where he wanted to build his home, and it turned out to be the area where the Melrose shopping center on Franklin Road now stands.

Rains and Robertson and the other first arrivals had not been there three months when the Indians struck. Their killings so terrorized the men that they could not go outside their fort to clear their fields unless they had other men guarding them with rifles.

Rains, who was thirty-six years old when he arrived at Fort Nashborough, was a high-tempered man who risked his life prodigiously, but he was protective toward his wife, Christiana, and their children. After seeing a steady increase in the attacks by "red rascals" in the spring of 1780, he bundled his family up and took them to the comparative peace of Kentucky to live till Nashborough was safe.

It was in the snowy January of 1781, on the way back from a trip to Kentucky, that he and a Mr. Stull, accompanying him, saw a band of Indians straight ahead. Rains turned his horse back, and the horse, followed by a pack horse, "jumped through a swinging grape vine," to avoid the Indians.

But Stull, on his horse, tried the same quick turn, and his horse was trapped on the grape vine, "swung right across it by the loins."

Stull hopped off the horse to disentangle him and took a moment to secure his "bag of provisions," strapped to the horse. But before he could remount the horse, "two Indians were running up," and Stull, who was "very fleet," started off on foot.

In the wild race, Rains caught two bullets through his

shirt and Stull darted off the path through the underbrush. Rains thought Stull had made his escape, "but shortly he heard one or two guns fired and then the yells of the Indians, then all was silent," as Rains's son told the story. "He knew Stull was dead."

Over sleet-covered snow, Rains made his way to a place where his horse could cross the swollen Green River. Rains, who could not swim himself, "tied his hunting shirt close around him, and rode in."

On the other side of the river, Rains used some of his gunpowder to set fire to a dried-out tree stump, and there he dried his icy clothes and warmed himself and his horse. On his lonely ride back toward Nashborough, Rains ran into James Robertson, also returning from a trip to Kentucky, where he had been sounding out prospects for help from Indian raids.

On January 15, 1781, the two men, along with two other companions, were ferried across the Cumberland at the Bluff (as they called Fort Nashborough), and the lookouts who saw them coming were so excited that they sent someone ahead to tell Robertson's wife and children, whom he had left in the care of friends at Freeland's Station (where 1400 Eighth Avenue, N. is today).

Rains spent the night at Fort Nashborough, but Robertson hurried to Freeland's Station (or fort) for a reunion with his wife and children, where he "rejoiced with them that they and he were yet alive."

For survival was a triumph then. And after a late supper, the usually closemouthed Robertson sat before the great fireplace and talked to the group there about what he had heard of the prospects for an end to the Revolutionary War and some hope of reinforcements and supplies.

Robertson shared with the men some of his new supply of gunpowder, bullets, and snuff, and before midnight the others went to sleep.

But there was no sleep for Robertson. Lying awake, listening, he heard movements outside the gate. His roaring cry of "Indians!" brought everybody in the fort to their feet, and their first thought was of the one log house along the fort's walls that "had not been completely chinked or daubed—there were large openings between the logs."

In that cabin, Major Lucas and a Negro servant of Robertson's were sleeping, along with other men. At the sound of Robertson's voice, Lucas rushed out of the cabin and was fatally wounded. Soon after that, a rifle pointing through the cracks killed Robertson's black servant.

"Those were the only fatal shots, although not less than 500 were fired into the house!" Tennessee historian John Haywood wrote.

Women in the fort said the screams of the Indians on the warpath were "like a thousand devils." "Possum" Hood, who saved his life once by playing dead while Indians scalped him, said there was certainly a "legion" of Indians surrounding Freeland's Station that night.

Meantime, at Fort Nashborough, John Rains, along with the others, heard the commotion at Freeland's, and the men at Nashborough fired their cannon—a weapon that terrified the Indians.

Long before daylight the battle was over, and the Indians had dragged their dead and wounded out of sight. Before daylight, Rains "came from the Bluff with a few trusty gunmen, a good supply of powder and ball, and earnest looking for the 'rascals'."

But the rascals were gone. And as they retreated, in a "scorched earth" tactic of their own, they burned grain in the fields and danced and screamed and whooped in ever-widening circles to scare away the great numbers of buffalo, deer, and bear on which the white settlers depended for food and clothes and sometimes shelter.

It was not just death, but the mutilating of victims that

horrified the white settlers. Some historians say that Joseph Hay—shot through the body, hacked with a hatchet, and scalped as he stopped for water at the Sulphur Spring—was the first white man killed by Indians at Nashville. Some say John Milliken, killed by Indians at the place where Charlotte crosses Richland Creek, was the first Indian victim.

Either way, it was the beginning of such slaughter that hundreds of early settlers turned to Kentucky for safety. They had seen the body of D. Larimer who was shot, scalped, and beheaded near Freeland's Station. They knew the way Isaac Lefevre, down on First Avenue, near Fort Nashborough, was "shot down, scalped and butchered" on the bluff overlooking the river.

They knew Solomon Philips, who was shot where Hume-Fogg high school stands now, at the corner of Eighth and Broad. He escaped to Fort Nashborough, but died of the wound in a few days. Solomon Murray, who was with Philips, was "killed on the spot, and scalped." And Robert Aspey was the third man killed at the present Eighth and Broad.

Fishing near the fort could mean death. Benjamin Renfroe, John Maxwell, and John Kennedy were fishing near Fort Nashborough when Indians "crept stealthily upon them, tomahawked and scalped Renfroe, who fought desperately, and made prisoners of the two others."

In those first few months in the Nashville area, there were over thirty deaths by Indians. In every instance, hot-tempered Rains was for "giving quick and hot pursuit." One day as two Fort Nashborough men fastened their canoe at the foot of the bluff and began climbing toward the fort, Indians appeared out of the bushes and shot at them.

Rains and two other men happened to be near and were able to rescue the white men. But that rescue developed into a fast-moving battle down by the Sulphur Spring, and Rains, with his rifle, saved another man from death and scalping there.

Danger was everywhere. A little girl whose family lived at Dunham's Station (where Belle Meade is now) ventured outside the stockaded walls to gather chips for her mother to cook supper. The child was scalped and her mother shot as she rushed out at the sound of the girl's screams.

Rains and Jacob Castleman took it upon themselves to "make a little hunt—just a little expedition—a sort of private affair," to avenge the attack on the child and her mother.

Following the trail of two or three Indians, Rains and Castleman "came quietly upon the heels of the rascals, and somehow 'Betsy' (Rains's gun) and 'Sister' (Castleman's gun) were both pointing at the Indians," historian A. W. Putnam tells the story.

The child survived the scalping and her mother survived the shot. But they were among the few lucky ones. And young Capt. James Leiper, first man to be married in Nashville, boasted at the wedding dinner about his encounters with Indians. He could not guess his fate when he rhymed: "The red-skin imp, I made him limp."

Leiper's marriage to Susan Drake was on April 30, 1780, and it was less than a year later, on April 2, 1781, that Leiper plunged Fort Nashborough into what was an almost disastrous fight with the Indians.

John Cotten, an aristocratic Virginian who had met James Robertson in Hillsborough, North Carolina, years before and joined him in the settlement at Fort Nashborough, kept a diary of those days of Indian horror, and his account of that April 2, 1781, fight (rather pompously called the Battle of the Bluff) is vivid.

The night before, guards in the watchtower at Fort Nashborough saw an Indian in the clearing outside the fort. And by morning it was evident that two young Indians "in war paint," firing their guns at a safe distance, laughing and taunting the guards, were trying to set a trap.

They knew enough English to scream insults at the guards, and young Leiper was "beside himself" with anger. He was all for attacking the Indians. But Robertson opposed it, and only reluctantly gave in to Leiper's pleading. Finally Robertson appointed twenty men, including himself, Leiper, Cotten, and John Rains, to ride out and rout the challenging Indians.

"We bade our wives and children farewell (I expected never to see mine again) and mounted up," Cotten wrote. "We rode out the gate with Jamie [Robertson] in the lead. The two Indians were at the edge of the clearing eastward of us [about where Broadway and Second is now], and when they saw us coming out they waved and vanished in the wood, going toward Cane Creek [now Demonbreun]."

The trap was so obvious that Robertson called Leiper back, but "the foolish lad" dashed into the wood where the two Indians had disappeared, and the nineteen other white men rushed forward to protect Leiper.

But when they reached the point where the Indians had disappeared (at about Third Avenue, between Broadway and Demonbreun), "about a score of Indians rose up out of the tall cane alongside the Creek . . . and laid a heavying firing on us, for which we were not in the least prepared."

The Indians were not, however, very good shots, some of them still fighting with bow and arrow and others just learning how to handle a rifle. And yet "poor Peter Gill was struck in the forehead by a ball and fell from his horse with his life's blood gushing as if a fountain."

Meantime half the Indians fell dead, and Robertson commanded his men to dismount and seek shelter. They slapped their horses and headed them toward the fort— they hoped.

And then suddenly "across the Creek such a multitude of warriors rose up out of the cane, I was hard put to keep from fleeing," Cotten admitted. "At the least, there were

300 of them, and they let go such a firing that the bark on both sides of my tree were cut off."

Cotten saw his friends falling about him, and when he sought cover in the underbrush and glanced up the hill toward the fort, he saw that they were cut off from there by "such a mass of Indians as I have never seen assembled in one place together . . .

"I crawled on my belly through the brush until I found Jamie [Robertson] and related to him what I had seen. Jamie called for all to withdraw, and at the edge of the wood we surveyed the scene with despair.

"Young Leiper, who had been so bold and eager to lead us into this foolhardy adventure, turned white as milk and said, 'Dear God.' " At that instant, the horses they had turned loose came crashing through the cane as the Indians tried to steal them, and they led the red men on a wild chase toward what is now the railroad gulch and up what is now Capitol Hill before they returned to the gate of the fort.

It was the one chance Robertson and his men had to make it back to the fort, and they made a dash for it. One of Robertson's men was killed with an arrow in his back as he ran.

"I let fire as fast as I could, though I have never been adept at loading while running, as John Rains is," Cotten wrote. "But I managed for the most part, save in close quarters, when I found my sword more effective."

Indians in pursuit were shooting and scalping as the white men ran up the hill toward the fort's gate, and then someone inside the fort opened the gate and let the dogs out, and the "ravening horde of dogs ran out and flew at the throats of the Indians.

"Such a sight has never been witnessed, for the confusion and noise is beyond words, men and beastes rolling together on the grass, screams of pain and cries of fear, blood flowing from torn throats, arms and legs," Cotten wrote.

Leiper was within sixty feet of the gate when an Indian's bullet tore through his body, and the stunned youth gasped for help. Cotten fought off Indians with his sword so that he could get Leiper inside to die in his young wife's arms.

Rains was one of the few who made it safely back to the fort, and next morning, "between Midnight and Sunup," he was one of the three men Robertson sent outside to "scout the Indians' whereabouts and to ascertain whether or no they be truly gone."

The three went in different directions, and Rains headed straight for Cane Creek where the fighting had begun the day before. Finding no Indians there, Rains dashed on out what is now Lebanon Road to Clover Bottom before he turned back to the fort.

Not only were there no Indians about, Rains reported, there were so many tracks of elk and buffalo that he "was all for going out and get them right now," Cotten said. "Jamie sobered him by asking if our dead yet remained where they fell."

Then the tireless Rains mounted his horse again and dashed off to see if there were any Indians to the west, and he found that they had withdrawn from the battle in such "great haste" that they "made no effort to cover up their path." At the point where Charlotte Road crosses Richland Creek, Rains stayed for some time, watching for signs of campfires.

He concluded that the "Indians were safely gone," and when he returned to the fort he astonished all by telling them that at least some of the Indians who had attacked were Chickasaws. Other scouts found that some of the warriors were Chickamaugas, the "renegade Cherokee."

And when it was safe, the men in the fort went outside to gather up the bodies of their dead, to bathe them and prepare them for burial, wrapped in buffalo robes.

"Gazing upon these poor corpses, whose lives had been so terribly ended for naught, I could not but gnash my teeth in anger and wish that I might strangle every savage in the land with my own bare hands," the usually calm Cotten wrote on Tuesday night, April 3, 1781.

"On the morrow we shall bury them. We shall weep for them, as we have for all those who have died, but we shall go on living, and one day we shall overcome this perilous wilderness."

But there were more battles to fight, following more Indian atrocities, and in 1787 Robertson again chose Rains, his "favorite scout," to lead fifteen men to an Indian village called Coldwater near the present Tuscumbia, Alabama.

Robertson assembled 130 men from the various forts around Nashville for the Coldwater expedition, and Rains and his men—sent to scout the territory and intercept the Indians at one point along the Tennessee River—handled their task so well that, according to one historian, they were "a body which for efficiency in border warfare was never surpassed."

The adventures of that one expedition could fill a book —scenes where scouts watched by moonlight young Indian warriors so confident that they playfully swung from dogwood trees to jump in the river; scenes in the sunlight where forty Indians stood in a canoe as it glided down the river; scenes where a young squaw jumped out of the canoe where she was held prisoner by the white men and let her clothes float away while she swam to safety on the opposite shore.

There were endless stories to tell of Indian raids in the Nashville area, and of Rains's last expedition, the Nickajack Expedition, in 1794. In his last days, he could be garrulous on the subject.

But after twenty-five years of fighting Indians, he settled down to the business of improving his vast farm operations. He had bought other land, and he had been one of the first to buy a lot in what is now downtown Nashville. That lot, covering almost half a block, runs along the southwest corner of Broadway and Sixth Avenue, where tour buses begin their tours today.

Rains grew bitter about lawyers after some litigation over his land, and doctors seemed unnecessary to early settlers, who never had pneumonia or neuralgia in spite of all their hardships. Rains summed it up:

"We used to think we had the devil to pay (and a heavy debt, too, running on long instalments) before the doctors and lawyers came; but the doctors introduced diseases, and the lawyers instituted suits, and now we have all to pay. Good health and harmony had prevailed until they came."

His sons and grandsons bought farms nearby, and some of them became leading citizens of the area. On part of their land is a hill still known as Rains Hill, and back of it for years was Rains Pond, where Nashville boys fished. Once there was a Rains School, and of course Rains Spring inside his old fort.

On his own original land grant, including the hill where the new television studio, WDCN (Channel 8), stands at 161 Rains Avenue today, Rains's sons and daughters and their husbands and wives built impressive homes. Streets in the neighborhood, like Merritt, Hamilton, and Hagan, are named for some of them who lived there. The old brick Hagan home still stands at the corner of Rains and Merritt, and the separate kitchen of the once grand Hamilton home is incorporated in a nearby house.

Nolensville Road cut diagonally across Rains's mile-square farm, and the high reaches of his land swept from the hills back of Rains Avenue across the broad valley along Brown's Creek and Nolensville Road and on up to the towering ridge where Ferro Glass Corporation has its sales offices (just off Polk Avenue) today.

On that ridge, with its magnificent view of downtown Nashville, parts of the old stone fences and mammoth gateposts that Rains's son and grandson had at their handsome homes still stand. One of the descendants, James S. Robinson, built a great house that he called Woodycrest at the present Ferro Sales Office site, and even now, in the spring, remnants of the old orchard and garden bloom. The name Woodycrest lives on in a street bordering the property.

It was on that same high ridge that Rains and his sons used to harvest their crops as they kept a sharp eye out for Indians. And it was obvious when John Rains died and his belongings were put up for sale that he had managed a thriving farm.

The sturdy Rains had not written a will and was ill only four days before he died at age ninety-one on March 26, 1834. He was buried first, it is said, at the old City Cemetery, near one corner of his farm, and it was not until 1893 that his remains were removed to Mt. Olivet Cemetery, on the lot of his Hagan descendants, in Section 13.

His wife, Christiana, had died in 1826, eight years before Rains. And their land, both on the farm and at the Broadway site, was divided eleven ways between Rains's children or their heirs. That land was divided by court decree on March 4, 1835.

Four months later, on July 11, 1835, Rains's household property and farm equipment and animals were sold. And the dozens of hogs, horses, oxen, stacks of fodder, barrels of corn, thousands of bushels of oats, wheat, and other grain were evidence of his farming skill.

His son Jonathan bought eight plows, six singletrees, scythes and cradles, pruning shears, and log chains. From the household furnishings, Jonathan bought silver trays and silverware, dishes and table cloths, fire irons, ovens, skillets and hooks, "one large table," one little table, one loom, sleigh and shuttle, and "all the lumber in the smoke house."

Gibson Merritt, son-in-law of Rains, bought "one large bowl, three large tablespoons, one young cow, one brown filley, 25 barrels of corn, one candle stand."

Timothy Demonbreun, son of the old French trader who was the first white man to spend a winter in Nashville, had married Rains's daughter, Christiana. They bought, among other things, "one whip saw and one large Bible."

Thomas Massey, who had married Rains's daughter Ursula, bought a few horses and ten bushels of wheat. Alfred P. Gowen, grandson of Rains, bought his grandfather's sword and "one large dish."

Others at the sale bought "one large falling leaf table," Windsor chairs, candlesticks, light stands. Dr. John Shelby bought 306 barrels of corn and "one large grindstone."

The day after the sale, according to county court records, the profits were divided between the eleven children or their heirs—$934 to each.

The old farm has changed hands many times since then, and the state fairgrounds—long a racetrack before it became a fairgrounds—is the largest pocket left of the old Indian scout's land.

It is safe to guess that if he could see the happy crowds at the fair, with the varied exhibits, Rains would be delighted. After all, that was part of what he was fighting the "red rascal" for—to make life safe for all men to enjoy.

Dr. John Shelby's Christmas Present

Nobody in Nashville ever found a gift under his Christmas tree quite like the one that young Dr. John Shelby received from his father in 1818.

John and his brother Anthony were presented 640 acres of choice land in what is now the heart of East Nashville, in a wide bend of the river opposite the Courthouse Square. Before the day was over, land-loving John had bought Anthony's portion of the land for $2,500.

And today Nashvillians touring that area—long called Edgefield—can see something of the influence that memorable gift of years ago has had on all of East Nashville.

Visitors today can reach back to 1785, to the Indian-fighting days in Sumner County when John Shelby was born—the first white child born in the county. Sightseers in East Nashville can still see evidence of the way Dr. Shelby worked to turn Nashville into a city of strong churches and schools, a city of great homes where hospitality overflowed in countless thoughtful ways.

The wedding reception that Dr. Shelby and his wife gave for their older daughter in 1827 was the talk of the town for weeks, and a visitor from South Carolina wrote of the elegance of the ball where Sam Houston danced and Andrew Jackson charmed the belles.

The three mansions that Dr. Shelby built in what is now East Nashville—one for himself and one for each of his two daughters—were constructed when his estate ran down to the river bank and stretched a mile up the slope.

He called two of the homes Fatherland—perhaps because they were built on the land his father had given him. The street named Fatherland in East Nashville took its name from one of those houses.

Another home—one that Dr. Shelby built for one of his daughters—was called Boscobel, and another East Nashville street took that name.

Shelby Street, Shelby Park, and the Shelby Street Bridge take their names from Dr. Shelby. Old maps of Nashville, showing the names of streets before they were changed to numbers, show further Shelby influence. Priscilla Street (now Ninth) was named for one of Shelby's daughters. Another daughter married G. Washington Barrow, and Barrow Street (now Second) was named for him. Dr. Shelby himself married a girl from Philadelphia whose last name was Minnick, and an East Nashville street was named Minnick for her family.

But Dr. Shelby's influence reached deeper than street names and parks and bridges. In the thick of politics, he was sometimes a confidant of Andrew Jackson and sometimes opposed him. He was the closest friend of Gov. Sam Houston when the latter resigned his office in despair after his bride of a few weeks mysteriously left him.

When others turned on the silent Houston, imagining that he had mistreated his bride, Dr. Shelby, good friend of both of them, stood staunchly by Houston.

It was perhaps that quality of loyalty, in addition to his enthusiasm for new enterprises, his sharp business sense, his zest for good living and fine horses and homes that made him one of the powers in the city's growth.

A slender, lean-faced man with dark hair and keen eyes, Dr. Shelby was quick to make decisions and impatient with second-rate work. He was horrified at the poor training that doctors in the Nashville area received, and angry at the poor care given wounded soldiers.

His own birth on the frontier, on May 24, 1785, brought on a minor crisis for a neighbor, George Blackmore, who dashed off to get a "granny woman" (midwife) to help in the delivery of the child.

Blackmore, "risking his life from lurking Indians and ruining a fine horse to go for a 'granny woman,' " said all that she brought with her was "a clean apron and her two hands"—plus her skill.

The young mother was charming Sarah Bledsoe Shelby, wife of David Shelby and daughter of that rugged frontier fighter and Revolutionary War soldier, Anthony Bledsoe. The infant, John Shelby, entering the world near the present Castalian Springs, in the thick of Indian raids, was to become prominent physician and wealthy citizen of Nashville, dispensing luxurious hospitality to hundreds of guests.

He was the first of twelve children of David and Sarah Shelby, and that young couple had just moved to Sumner County on their wedding trip the year before. David had fought as a teenager in the Revolutionary War, fighting alongside his father and his cousin, Col. Isaac Shelby, in the famous Battle of King's Mountain.

Isaac Shelby, one of the towering figures on the frontier, became the first governor of Kentucky, and it was for him that Shelby County, Tennessee, (with Memphis as county seat) and Shelbyville were named.

Isaac Shelby, along with Anthony Bledsoe, helped lay off the land in the Cumberland area that was to be given to Revolutionary War soldiers in recognition of their services. That was the same Anthony Bledsoe whose daughter married David Shelby before they set out for Sumner County on horseback to claim their land.

When David and his bride finally chose the site for their home, it was the land prized above all others by Thomas

Sharp ("Big Foot") Spencer, one of the legendary explorers of Middle Tennessee.

Spencer, a fearless hunter and Indian fighter, a giant of a man whose feats of strength frightened Indians and white men alike, had such big feet that Indians tracking him turned back in terror.

Others in a hunting party of white men exploring the Middle Tennessee forests in 1778 turned homeward when winter approached. But Spencer, the loner, the man who loved the silence of the woods, chose to remain alone in Sumner County that winter—the first white man ever to spend a winter in the area.

Spencer made his home inside the hollow trunk of a giant sycamore tree near the present huge log house called Wynnewood, at Castalian Springs, while he cleared the land for the first crop in the region.

And when he made his choice of all the land available to him, he staked out a 640-acre tract of rich land on rolling hills about one mile southwest of Gallatin's downtown area. From that moment on, the land was known as Spencer's Choice.

But before Spencer could build his home there, he was killed by Indians as he returned from a journey to Virginia in 1794.

Soon afterward, David Shelby bought the land called Spencer's Choice and began work on the stone house with its walls two feet thick and its fine paneling and other distinctive millwork. That house, always called Spencer's Choice, was completed in 1798 and stood until the 1960s, when it was torn down to make way for a subdivision.

Several of David Shelby's twelve children were born in that hospitable stone home—center of a prosperous farm where famous men of the day were often guests.

John, the oldest of the children, was thirteen years old when the family moved into the house. One of his younger sisters, Nellie, was born there in 1799, shortly after the family moved in. It was Nellie whose granddaughter, Alva Erskine Smith, married William Kissam Vanderbilt, son of the founder of Vanderbilt University, "Commodore" Cornelius Vanderbilt.

And it was Alva's son, Harold S. Vanderbilt, who served as chairman of the board of trust at Vanderbilt in recent years. His sister, Consuelo Vanderbilt, married the Duke of Marlborough, cousin of Winston Churchill.

At Spencer's Choice there was obvious emphasis on solid schooling, and when John Shelby was ready to enter medical school he traveled to Philadelphia to enter the medical school of the University of Pennsylvania and study under the most famous physician and teacher of the day, Dr. Benjamin Rush.

Signer of the Declaration of Independence and leader in Philadelphia's social and medical world, Dr. Rush was a power in the nation's political circles. And John Shelby— twenty-two years old when he entered medical school in 1807—was soon swept up in the city's social whirl. There he met Anna Mariah Minnick, daughter of a prominent Philadelphia family, and they were married a few months after his graduation from medical school in 1809.

Dr. John Shelby began his medical practice in Sumner County that same year, in the Gallatin area. He and his wife were still living there in 1813 when their first child, Ann, was born, and in 1815, when their second daughter, Priscilla, was born.

But in 1813, Dr. Shelby went off to war, serving under Gen. Andrew Jackson, to put an end to the massacres inflicted on hundreds of white settlers by Creek Indians in Alabama and Tennessee.

In that campaign, Dr. Shelby was disgusted with the poor care that wounded soldiers received from doctors who had scant training. Poorly trained doctors were responsible for the death of many soldiers, he believed.

As he tended the wounded near the battlefront, Dr. Shelby lost an eye. General Jackson, pushed for men to aid in battle, paid high tribute to the valuable care Shelby and his assistants had given. "The whole staff deserve my thanks," Jackson wrote Shelby.

From Huntsville, Alabama, near Fort Deposit, on February 17, 1814, Dr. Shelby wrote General Jackson about the miserable conditions at the army post. In the winter cold, there was no shelter for the sick men but tents.

"I was astonished to find the sick were in their respective tents," Shelby reported. "Upon inquiring into the case, there were no tools to scrub a house or houses for their accommodation."

Shelby had been assured that men were on the way to build suitable houses, "but Hospital stores are extremely scarce."

His compassion for the sick and the helpless was a life-long prod to activity. When the war was over and his terms in the state senate in 1815 and 1817 failed to produce legislation requiring certain standards for practicing physicians, he did not give up the fight.

He moved to Nashville in 1817, after buying a home at the corner of the present Fourth and Charlotte avenues on May 17, 1817. He paid $6,000 for that house on the northwest corner of the intersection, and was living there the next year when his father, David, tied a red ribbon—figuratively speaking—around a huge chunk of East Nashville and gave it to his two oldest sons for a Christmas present.

It was on December 21, 1818, that David Shelby made the presentation. It was land the wealthy father of the doctor had owned since 1788 when its first owner, James Shaw, sold it to get away from Indian raids that were terrorizing the Nashville area.

The exact border of the land in that Christmas present is not clear today. Maps showing the parcel of land in 1786 make it look much larger than 640 acres. Following the outlines of that early map of the area, it would seem that John Shelby's land was like a slice of pie—with the curve of the river making the round side of the slice, and the two straight sides running along the present South Fourteenth Street on one side and along the present Berry Street on the other.

But if the parcel of land was indeed 640 acres, map experts say, the slice of pie would be bound by South Seventh Street on one side and Main Street on the other. Either way, it included much of what later was called Edgefield.

James Shaw had operated a ferry between his land and the Public Square, and David Shelby became owner of the ferry when he bought the Shaw farm. Shelby continued to operate the ferry for the thirty years he owned it, and then he and his son, Dr. Shelby, organized a company to build the first bridge across the Cumberland, connecting East and West Nashville.

That covered bridge, a sturdy stone structure, was opened in 1822, connecting the northeast corner of the Courthouse Square with the Gallatin turnpike on the other side of the river.

It was only because heavy steamboat traffic later made it necessary to have a higher bridge that Dr. Shelby and his father replaced the covered bridge with a graceful suspension bridge, opened in 1855. Designed by noted architect Adolphus Heiman (the same architect who designed at least one of Dr. Shelby's mansions in East Nashville), that new toll bridge was still earning an income for the two Shelbys when they died.

Dr. Shelby's "Christmas present" land, rising above a wide curve in the Cumberland, offered dramatic settings for the handsome homes he built there. The first of those homes sat squarely in what is now Woodland Street, between Second and Third streets.

That first home, completed in the early 1820s, was the setting for the elaborate wedding of his daughter, Ann, on September 27, 1827. That wedding, the biggest social event of the season, had Nashville people talking for months.

The bride was only fourteen, and daughter of the richest man in Nashville. The groom, a handsome young man just nineteen years old, had just graduated from the University of Nashville and was ready to begin his law practice.

The diary of a fashionable young woman from Charleston, South Carolina, in Nashville with her wealthy husband on a combination wedding and business trip, gives a vivid description of Ann Shelby's wedding and the notables who attended.

Juliana Conner and her husband Henry Workman Conner were entertained at the Hermitage and other great homes of the area (see "Partying in Nashville in 1827"). She wrote of having tea at the home of Maj. and Mrs. Henry Rutledge (on what is now Rutledge Hill, in South Nashville) and hearing much chatter about the coming wedding.

"One of the topics of conversation last evening was relative to a splendid wedding, to take place on Thursday—daughter of Dr. Shelby, one of the wealthiest men in Nashville," Juliana wrote in September, 1827.

"The preparations for it have been unparalleled—making additions to the house, cutting windows, doors, etc., 500 cards of invitations issued—in fact the whole body politic and corporate of the city."

Gov. Sam Houston was to be an attendant at the wedding, and he brought invitations to the Conners, "so I shall behold at one time and place all the beauty, fashion and splendor of the city."

General Jackson may have been an attendant also, since he went ahead of his wife and was helping put guests at ease at the reception. Mrs. Jackson sent word to Juliana Conner that she would come by the Nashville Inn (on the Public Square) so that they could drive together to the wedding in East Nashville.

That Thursday morning, September 27, dawned clear and cool, and Juliana Conner wrote of the city's excitement.

"Thus was the important day," she wrote, "great in the annals of the fashionable world—anticipated with delight by many a youthful beauty and gay gallants—as the scene of their triumph and display. Even the old and grave men were not exempt from pleasing expectations in mingling with the festive throng."

Andrew Jackson's wife arrived in town early for the drive to Shelby Hall, as Dr. Shelby called that first home for a few years. When Juliana Conner and Mrs. Jackson arrived, they were "ushered into a drawing room filled with ladies soon after we entered (and before one fifth of the company had assembled.)"

The bride was "really quite pretty and I dare not say her charms were heightened by the aid of a rich and elegant dress," Juliana wrote. The wedding "form" was Presbyterian, "very short," and after the bride and groom received congratulations they and their attendants left the room. In the ballroom, after supper, Juliana said it was a "fashionable squeeze unprecedented."

The most charming man at the reception, Juliana said, was General Jackson—"certainly a most superior man. His most trifling actions and expressions indicate it . . . "

That was a year before Jackson was elected president. It was fourteen years before the bridegroom would rise to prominence in the James K. Polk administration, serving as minister to Portugal. He too would be elected to Congress, in 1847.

It was for this bride and groom, Ann and Washington

Barrow, that Dr. Shelby built a stately home a few blocks east of his home. That house, with white-columned entrances on three sides, was called Boscobel (meaning "beautiful woods").

Meantime, Dr. Shelby changed the name of his home from Shelby Hall to Fatherland. Later, when he built another home a few blocks away, he named it Fatherland also.

But it was at the first Fatherland (where Woodland Street is now) that he spent most of his life, and the letters he wrote to statesmen, doctors, church leaders, horse breeders, and other friends were always headed "Fatherland."

It was because the Woodland Street bridge led traffic practically to his front door that Dr. Shelby decided to build a new home several blocks eastward (at what was later 701 South Fifth). That home, later used as a Florence Crittenden Home for unwed mothers, was designed by Adolphus Heiman, the same noted architect who designed the suspension bridge, according to Mrs. Margaret M. Ikenberry (in a paper on Dr. Shelby in *Send for a Doctor,* published in 1975 by Nashville's public library).

Mrs. Ikenberry states that Shelby, seventy years old when that second Fatherland was built in 1855, intended it as a home for his daughter Priscilla (married first to David Williams and later to Judge John D. Phelan).

Mrs. Ikenberry describes the second Fatherland as a "stately house sitting on 20 acres of wooded grounds . . . with iron fence and high gates, always closed and locked each night." There were marble mantels, handsome chandeliers, hand-blocked wallpaper, and Aubusson rugs.

In 1857, sophisticated world traveler and mayor of Nashville Randal McGavock described Dr. Shelby's new home as "better adapted for a fine entertainment than any other in the state."

McGavock had just attended a 5 o'clock dinner and

dance at the Shelby home the night before and he said they "kept up the dance until a very late hour."

At that very moment, there was a group of doctors forming a new medical school here, and they would name it for one of its sponsors, Dr. Shelby. It would open in the fall of 1858, with its building facing on Broad Street, between Seventh and Eighth avenues, where the old Federal Building stands today.

Shelby Medical College was occupied by Federal forces during the Civil War and was so wrecked that it was never reopened. But its faculty later formed Vanderbilt School of Medicine.

A joiner, Dr. Shelby was not only active in local and national medical associations; he was also one of a small group who founded Nashville's first Episcopal church (Christ Church) in 1825. Later, in 1856, he gave the land in East Nashville for St. Ann's Episcopal Church.

Along with Andrew Jackson, Gen. William Carroll, and other prominent men of his day, he helped form the first Jockey Club in Nashville in 1816. In some of his last letters, written in 1858, he described a fine horse he was willing to sell ("I value him at $1,000").

When Dr. Shelby died at age seventy-four, on May 15, 1859, there were profuse tributes from the medical profession and the city at large. The faculty of the Shelby Medical College made up one group attending the funeral at Christ Episcopal Church. The funeral procession to the old City Cemetery included colorfully uniformed "Shelby Life Guards" and German "Yagers." The lands he had developed, the friends he had won were almost beyond counting.

And few in the crowd had any idea that his imprint on the city began with a magnificent Christmas present from his father so long ago.

George Deaderick,
Banker in Knee Pants

When First American National Bank opened its new twenty-eight-story building in the heart of downtown Nashville for the first time on July 30, 1973, the historic site was peopled with memories.

There the great men of the state's early days—Andrew Jackson, Sam Houston, James K. Polk, Andrew Johnson, among others—argued, bought goods, signed notes, headed long parades.

There the city's richest man at the time, George Michael Deaderick, hardfisted president of the state's first bank, did business. For, by coincidence, the very spot where the new First American National Bank stands is property once owned by that pioneer banker.

And that banker gave the land for Deaderick Street, the street (named for him) that now welcomes customers to the tower side of the new bank.

George M. Deaderick, straight out of Revolutionary War days, looked like a short, plump version of George Washington. In knee pants, with buckles at the knees, and powdered hair tied in a cue at the nape of his neck, he was, to Nashvillians, the picture of a "Virginia gentleman."

When the thirty-two-year-old Deaderick arrived here from his native Virginia in 1788, Tennessee was still part of North Carolina. And that same year a young North Carolina lawyer, red-haired Andrew Jackson, arrived at Nashville—a dirty village "of two taverns, two stores, one distillery, one courthouse and a fringe of cabins, bark tents and wagon camps," all fenced in to keep "browsing buffalo at a distance."

In 1784, four years before Deaderick and Jackson arrived, the Town of Nashville was incorporated and its name changed from the British-sounding Nashborough to the more acceptable French form, Nashville. After all, the French had helped the colonies fight the British.

Deaderick and Jackson had both suffered loss of members of their family in the Revolutionary War. Both of them lost no time in making their fortunes in Nashville, the frontier town clustered around a log courthouse on the Public Square.

Deaderick was soon amassing a fortune as wholesale merchant, real estate man, and banker. He not only lent money to Jackson to go into business for himself, but also felt so close to Jackson that he turned to the statesman—almost disastrously—for advice on how to stop Mrs. Deaderick from flirting.

Deaderick, member of a distinguished family of senators, congressmen, bankers, and judges (one nephew, James William Deaderick, was chief justice of the Tennessee Supreme Court from 1875 to 1886), had a brother, David, who was president of a bank at Jonesboro.

Their German-born father, David Dietrich of Wurtemburg, had arrived in the United States in 1747. After a few years in Philadelphia, David Dietrich (he soon changed the spelling to the Anglicized form, Deaderick) moved to Winchester, Virginia.

There George Michael Deaderick and several of the other children in the family were born. And apparently the Deadericks never lost their Virginia accents and manners.

George Michael Deaderick, even in his latter days, clung to the old colonial habits of dress.

"He wore fair top boots, short pants with knee buckles,

swallow or cutaway coat, and the cue of his hair hanging at the back of his neck was slightly powdered," one of his relatives wrote years later.

"All of that to us at the present day would present a quaint appearance, but it was then the fashion with many elderly gentlemen, and as familiar as our dress of today."

Deaderick, a cocky little man (five feet, six inches tall), "rather heavily built, full florid face, composed in expression, manners grave, and self-possessed in his movements," wasted no time in getting in on Nashville's first business boom.

Indians were still scalping people who ventured far without guns, but the brave little Town of Nashville was laid out, in 1784, in long blocks ranged along each side of the Public Square and extending several blocks in three directions.

Deaderick bought Lot No. 39—half the area now covered by the new First American National Bank. That lot ran from Union Street to Deaderick, and from Third Avenue to Printers Alley.

It was George Deaderick, in fact, who donated to the Town of Nashville the land for Printers Alley—as a service entrance for businesses that fronted on Third and Fourth (then called Cherry).

And Deaderick's gift of a thoroughfare through his property, running from the Public Square to what is now Memorial Square, was rewarded by a grateful Nashville. The town named the street in Deaderick's honor. That street name is the only reminder that Deaderick ever lived here.

For almost half of its ninety-year history, the bank conducted business in the handsome gray stone building that closed its doors to customers for the last time in 1973. That substantial building, with its rounded entrance at the corner of Fourth and Union, was demolished, and in its place was built a wide-sweeping, landscaped plaza to front the bank's new amber-colored skyscraper.

That wide plaza reminds history buffs that just across Deaderick Street there was once a blooming garden, adjacent to the home of George Deaderick's youngest brother, Thomas. Thomas Deaderick, also a merchant, was, like his banker brother, "well known as an honest and upright man and had the esteem and confidence of the citizens and surrounding country."

Thomas Deaderick and his wife, Eliza, lived in "a frame cottage" near their garden, close to the west side of the Public Square. Adjoining the other side of the garden was Nashville's "first brick residence, built in 1805 and called the Mansion House," Miss Jane Thomas, one of the city's early residents, wrote.

That was the area where Nashville began. That was the area where famous visitors, like General Lafayette and numerous presidents, were entertained. Oddly enough, in the early days Union Street was only an eight-foot-wide alley.

What is today the "Wall Street of the South" was then Union Alley. The new First American National Bank has its main entrance on still-narrow Union Street.

George M. Deaderick owned many downtown lots, and knew that neighborhood as few men have. Grim-faced and rosy-cheeked, he paced off his long lots that reached back 174 feet from Third Avenue to Printers Alley.

He soon built a fine home in the country. By 1804, Deaderick had prospered so that he owned several tracts of farmland in the Brown's Creek area, on what is now Franklin Road. That year he built on his Brown's Creek plantation (on a hill overlooking what is now the Melrose shopping center) a two-story white frame mansion with square columns across the front and wrought-iron trim across the second-floor balcony.

But Deaderick's wealth brought little happiness, even in the big white house at the top of the hill. Jackson, who had bought fifty shares in Deaderick's bank, the Bank of Nashville, soon found out how devoid of happiness Deaderick's life was.

For one thing, Deaderick's giddy wife loved worrying her husband by flirting with other men—using her eyes with "much levity and viciousness," as he put it.

She gave parties and went to dances often—usually without bothering to get her husband's consent. Sometimes he was off in Philadelphia, buying merchandise for his wholesale merchandising business in Nashville. Piteously the hard-boiled Deaderick turned to his old friend Jackson (who bought supplies from Deaderick for his own store) to ask how *he* would handle the situation.

Deaderick, in fact, asked Jackson to go to the banker's home and have a talk with Mrs. Deaderick about how much she was worrying her husband by her flirtations. The Deadericks were separated, and the banker wanted a reconciliation with his wife.

Reluctantly Jackson agreed to the mission. In sorrow, he learned the futility of it. After the visit, Mrs. Deaderick helped spread gossip that Jackson had made improper advances to her. He had, she implied, "had carnal knowledge" of her.

Poor Deaderick, knowing well his wife's tricks, came to Jackson's defense. He knew his wife had made up the whole story. On April 25, 1807, Deaderick wrote a long letter of apology to Jackson for ever having involved him in the effort to make "eternal reconciliation between Mrs. D and myself."

Deaderick's wife's parents had made a terrible scene about the whole thing, and Deaderick had fled to escape their wrath. If her parents "advocate the going to private dances, in and out of Town Assemblys, inviting Gentlemen & Ladies to my house, all without my knowledge or consent . . . the principal shall never be approved of by me," Deaderick wrote Jackson.

"By the expression of the eye, as much levity & Vicious-ness can be expressed as the tongue is capable of uttering, and as strong declarations made, and as easily under-stood."

Deaderick denied any jealousy. He said his "heart was transported with joy" when he saw her "engaged in inno-cent Amusement, and reputable society." But he would not end his separation from his wife, he said, until she mended her ways.

Two years later, on March 5, 1809, writing from his Brown's Creek plantation, Deaderick told Jackson that he had found out who the gossips were who were trying to stir up dissension among both Deaderick and Jackson kin. Deaderick said he would never believe the stories the gos-sips were circulating.

"My knowledge of you for many years . . . your rectitude forbad the impression," fifty-three-year-old Deaderick wrote Jackson, forty-two, who had already served as con-gressman, senator, state supreme court justice, and major general in the militia.

Deaderick himself had opened the Bank of Nashville two years before, in 1807. He was immensely proud of the fact that it was the first bank in Tennessee, and that Jackson was a stockholder.

"Your friendship for me I have long known and have held dear to my heart," Deaderick continued in the 1809 letter of apology to Jackson, "and I do at this moment . . . My esteem for you has been uniform and remains unabat-ed . . .

"Your recent exertions to restore harmony between Mrs. Deaderick and myself call for my warmest acknowledge-ment. The desire of my heart has been that you should be instrumental to effect the first object of my wish—peace with a companion whose friendly converse has often been balm to my Soul."

Not only was Mrs. Deaderick stirring up trouble among relatives and friends by making false statements about their conduct toward her; she also accused Deaderick's numerous nieces and nephews of trying to get some of his money.

Every time a new baby in the Deaderick family was named for the banker-uncle, Mrs. Deaderick said there was a mercenary motive.

"Mrs. Dk ... with much ill nature ... signified that the child was named after me with a view that it might inherit my property," the rich banker wrote Jackson.

The marriage ended in divorce, and Mrs. Deaderick remarried.

Six years later, when Jackson had become a national hero by defeating the British in the Battle of New Orleans, Nashville citizens gave a ball in his honor at Talbot's Inn on the Public Square, in May, 1815. And George M. Deaderick was chairman of the committee making the arrangements.

The ball, they notified Jackson, was "to testify their gratitude to you for your Service and their Joy at your safe return to Tennessee."

Deaderick, the unhappy banker, was "hospitable, kind and considerate in his intercourse with others," a friend wrote. "A man not easily influenced in his opinion of men and things, and steadily adhering to them when once formed, upholding what he considered to be right, and opposing what he thought wrong.

"He was honest, just and humane."

His spacious country home, named Westwood by later owners (Westwood Avenue took its name from the house), was said to be the second oldest home on Franklin Road (only Travelers Rest was older). Made of big wooden blocks painted white, the house was torn down perhaps as late as 1970, to make way for a highway.

It stood on the crest of a hill just back of the spot where

Melrose Camera Center is today. The lot where it stood is vacant, a jungle of vines and weeds knitting the ancient trees in thick oblivion.

But when the plantation was in its prime and Deaderick rode his horse or took his carriage to town, to his bank, he was a model of success and prosperity. He was the town's richest man. He was so proud of his bank that the only thing he wanted on his tombstone (in the quarter-acre family graveyard near the garden on his Brown's Creek plantation) was his name and the title "President of the Bank of Nashville."

In 1814, two years before his death, Deaderick began leasing lots in the half-block area stretching from Third Avenue to Printers Alley. They were ninety-nine-year leases, and the rent for each lot was to be $250 per year.

Witnesses to his will, written on November 15, 1816, included Felix Robertson, distinguished son of Nashville's founder, James Robertson.

Deaderick had a young son, John George M. Deaderick, to whom he willed $15,000, and an adopted son, Fielding Deaderick, to whom he willed $10,000. Both were minors at the time the sixty-year-old Deaderick wrote his will.

Numerous nieces and nephews were to share in the fortune, and Deaderick's death, probably in December, 1816, was signal to years of litigation.

By 1822, one of the lots that Deaderick had leased for $250 per year sold for $1,610. Joseph Litton bought it. That same year, Thomas Yeatman bought one of Deaderick's adjoining lots (on the present bank site) for $2,201, and Judge John McNairy bought the next one for $2,075.

By the time all of Deaderick's lots had been sold, the total value was $79,392. By the time the executors of the estate and the lawyers got their share, the estate had dwindled, in 1832, to $39,055.

Litton, in 1832, deeded the property where part of the

new bank stands today to W. B. Cooper "to settle debts." On the lots at that time were "storehouse and outbuild- ings."

On the day after Christmas, 1846, the lots and buildings were sold at public auction for $14,900. By 1874, the prop- erty belonged to Daniel E. Carter, and in his will, dated February 23, 1874, he left it to his wife and daughter, Rachel A. Craighead (wife of Thomas D. Craighead).

Rachel Craighead, in her will, dated December 17, 1912, left her share of the old Deaderick property to her cousin, John C. Buntin, and his wife, Elizabeth.

But long before that, Deaderick's Bank of Nashville had disappeared. Many others had come and gone. And in 1883 —almost a century after George Deaderick arrived on the Nashville scene—a new bank was founded: First American National Bank.

And George Deaderick, who gave the street to the city and worked hard to build its financial future, lives again in the new financial center.

Otherwise, all trace of Deaderick here is gone. Fortune, family, home, and grave have vanished.

But in the 1890s, when Deaderick's old home, West- wood, was in caring hands, the graveyard that he had set aside for the burial of many members of the family was still visible. Even then, relatives wrote, Deaderick's tombstone was "covered with moss, ivies and decayed leaves, and the stone is crumbling. The only legible inscription on it is the name, 'George Michael Deaderick, President of the Bank of Nashville.' "

Earthquake Opens "Fountain of Health"

The "Fountain of Health" burst out of a ripped hillside near the Hermitage one December night in 1811 while Nashville rocked in a terrifying earthquake.

It was the same tremor that temporarily changed the course of the Mississippi River and created Reelfoot Lake in West Tennessee.

Although no traces are left today of the "miraculous waters" that appeared only a mile east of the Hermitage, they were a sensation at the time.

In an era when mineral springs were the rage, these waters fairly dripped with chemicals from the earth's crust.

A thriving health resort blossomed on the spot, and flourished for fifteen years. The lame and ailing came from as far away as New Orleans and the Virginia coast.

The owner and promoter, an enterprising lawyer named William Saunders, advertised the waters as a cure for everything from sore eyes and ulcerated skin to rheumatism, asthma, stomach disorders, "warts and tetterworms and wens on the wrists."

One patient, once the richest girl in Virginia, came to the Fountain of Health to take the cure for dope addiction. She was the lovely young Anne McCarty Lee, wife of the tragic "Black Horse Harry" Lee. Lee was the older half brother of Confederate Gen. Robert E. Lee.

Out of Anne Lee's stay at the Fountain of Health—and the spring's proximity to the Hermitage—came Harry

85

Lee's close association with Andrew Jackson, both during the presidential campaign and at the White House.

It was sheer luck that the earth happened to rip open and create the spring on land owned by one of Davidson County's sharpest operators.

Saunders, who had come from Gates County, North Carolina, had bought the 193-acre farm just east of the Hermitage in December, 1807. He paid $10 an acre for the tract which spilled over into Wilson County, as deeds at the courthouse show.

Saunders was farming the land and practicing law when the earthquake struck, about 2:15 on Monday morning, December 16, 1811.

"The shocks which continued until after day were some of them very severe—so much so that the heaviest houses seemed to be racked to pieces," the *Democratic Gazette and Clarion* reported the next day.

"However, we have heard of no real injury sustained except the fall of some chimneys in the country ... This being the first shock of the kind ever felt in the place and commencing at the hour it did, terrified the citizens at first very much, until recollection assigned the true cause of the dreadful visitation."

But it wasn't all dreadful, Saunders soon discovered. Below the hill where his house stood, the earth had cracked open to reveal a rushing spring with a strong sulphur and mineral taste. He began experimenting with its medicinal qualities.

The earth tremors continued through the winter of 1811–12. By July, 1813, Saunders was open for business. He had turned his farm home into a health resort and advertised that he was building more cottages for guests.

The Clarion and Tennessee Gazette ran his first ad on July 13, 1813. It began with a description of the violent birth of the spring:

"Immediately after the tremendous Earth Quakes which visited our land in the winter of 1811 and 1812 and shocked our Earth to the very centre, a stream of purest Mineral Water broke forth from the bowels of the Earth on the plantation of the subscriber, which the All Wise Providence in his unbounded goodness and mercy seems to have intended as a peculiar blessing to mankind."

The ad spoke of the "great number of experiments which have been made upon persons variously affected," and said that "in no instance whatever has it failed to give more or less relief, and in most of them perfectly restored the patient to the highest health—contrary to the belief and expectations of all who saw them, which induces a belief that it is a fountain of Universal Medicine."

Saunders followed up with sworn testimonials to the benefits of his cure-all.

There was, for instance, General Overton's son, who was "cured of a very bad sore in four days constant application of this water, which had for some time baffled the General's skill."

All the way from Natchez, Mississippi, came William Ewell, who had suffered "upwards of four years with the intermitting fever" and whom doctors had supposed "to be at death's door." Ewell said he was so ill that he "came to Tennessee with considerable difficulty" and was so weak when he arrived that he could hardly make it from the resort hotel to the spring 150 yards down the hill.

But after ten days of drinking and bathing in water from the Fountain of Health, he was again a "healthy and hearty man."

Thomas A. Oden, who lived near Nashville, stated in a testimonial that he had suffered for about a year from a "complaint of the bowels" and was "reduced very low" when he went to the Fountain of Health. After two weeks there, he was cured.

One Negro man, "who was ulcerated from the crown of his head to the sole of his feet . . . insomuch that a finger could be thrust into many places about his head, shoulders, elbows and legs" was "healed of this putrefaction entirely from the drinking and washing in this water."

Saunders's ad stated that he had had the water analyzed, and had determined that it contained "Chalybeate and sulphur," and was believed by doctors to be "impregnated with a kind of salts and Magnesia."

The story of the Fountain of Health came to light again about 1967 when Syd Houston Hailey, a retired civil engineer for the N. C. & St. L. Railway, began tracing his wife's family history. Mrs. Hailey, the former Mary Margaret Saunders, turned out to be a great-granddaughter of William Saunders, Sr., owner of the Fountain of Health.

Much research has turned up old deeds, wills, and family records referring to the property. Hailey was impressed with Saunders's salesmanship.

Saunders changed his rates at the Fountain of Health as it grew in popularity. In 1813, when the resort opened, he charged five dollars a week to board a man and his horse. If a guest paid by the day, the charge was one dollar.

Two years later, Saunders was pushing the Fountain of Health as a summer resort "situated in the most sociable neighborhood known in all the country—four miles East from the Clover Bottom, and 14 miles above the town of Nashville."

By that time, he had built "an excellent ice house" and had "safely deposited within its walls 1200 bushels of ice." That meant plenty of ice cream and iced drinks for guests. That same year, 1815, he added to the main building and the rows of guest cottages around it "a very convenient and agreeable Summer dancing room."

But the emphasis was still on restoring health.

"There are but few diseases that flesh is heir to in which

some relief has not been experienced," he advertised in Nashville newspapers.

By 1819, the Fountain of Health was booming and rates jumped to nine dollars a week. The main road from Nashville to Lebanon—an old stagecoach road much traveled not only by local residents but also by politicians on their way to Knoxville and Washington—was changed to go by the resort.

Sam A. Weakley, a retired civil engineer and amateur historian, made a special project in the 1930s of determining the exact course of the old road that was rerouted by the Fountain of Health. He said the roadbed has been completely obliterated by lots in a subdivision east of the Hermitage now.

Saunders, in his ads, stated that the road that came to his door was "the best road from Nashville to Lebanon." He directed travelers from Nashville to turn off on it "at Cherry's, near Clover Bottom." Travelers from Lebanon were to turn "at the Eagle Tavern."

In 1824 a post office was established at the Fountain of Health, and mail from Washington to Andrew Jackson and his neighbors was addressed simply to the "Fountain of Health, Tenn."

As a neighbor and admirer of Andrew Jackson, Saunders named his youngest son for the general in 1823, long before Jackson became president.

It may have been Saunders who introduced one of his most distinguished guests, Mrs. Henry Lee of Virginia, to Rachel and Andrew Jackson. At any rate, Mrs. Lee, one of the saddest figures in history, became Rachel's devoted friend while she was "taking the cure."

Mrs. Lee, an heiress who had entertained elegantly at the Lee mansion at Stratford, had lost family, fortune, home. A scandal that rocked Virginia society had separated her from her ill-starred husband, "Black Horse Harry" Lee.

It was about 1825 when the bereft Mrs. Lee—only twenty-seven at the time—came to the Fountain of Health to cure herself of the dope habit. She soon met Rachel Jackson, whose kindness and encouragement—perhaps more than the medicinal waters at the resort—restored Anne McCarty Lee to a new hold on life.

Rachel and Andrew Jackson are credited with reuniting Anne Lee and her long-estranged husband, and the Lees lived for a time at the Fountain of Health. Later they lived at a home about 2½ miles from Nashville, on the road to the Hermitage.

The Lees were with Jackson at Rachel's funeral. They went with him to Washington and Lee continued as Jackson's secretary when the latter was in the White House.

Meantime Saunders—apparently because of his excessive claims for the cure-all waters—had run into trouble.

He stated in an ad in April, 1823, that he could understand why "uninformed" people would find the claims hard to believe. To try to prove his own confidence, he offered a guarantee: "No cure, no pay."

Saunders had been advertising his Fountain of Health as cure for "ulcers of the liver, gonorrhea, jaundice—some of the most difficult diseases, which for many Centuries has baffled the skill in medicine."

He issued thanks to the public for their patronage of this "extraordinary fountain of Medicinal water," with its "efficacious effect upon almost all the complaints that fall to the share of humanity."

Three years later, in an ad in *The Nashville Banner and Nashville Whig,* he was far more cagey:

"I have made no preparations, nor ever shall again, to invite visitors to this Fountain," he stated on May 10, 1826, just as the summer season was about to open. "But I will never deny its benefit and a decent accommodation to the afflicted.

"Nor will I receive any compensation from any person unless the benefit is commensurate in any of the following diseases: all bowel complaints, affections of the liver, dyspepsia, rheumatism, ulcers, gonorrhea, wens, warts and tetters and for all irregularities incident to the delicate female."

By 1832 he was identifying the location as next door to "the Hermitage, President Jackson's seat."

That year he advertised a new invention, the "water railway"—a system of ropes and pulleys by which water could be hauled from the spring at the foot of the hill to the resort quarters above, all in two minutes, "with the help of a little boy."

Saunders was still at the Fountain when he died at age seventy, in 1846, one year after his neighbor Jackson's death.

None of Saunders's four sons (three of them lawyers) or four daughters was interested in operating the place.

In time, the earth presumably filled in the earthquake-born spring, and eventually tilled soil covered every trace of it.

The old house and all the cottages were torn away long before the memory of anyone living today, but in the 1930s Sam Weakley found a few bricks from the foundation.

Out of the plowed field came an old rock biscuit block where biscuits were once beaten for guests at the Fountain of Health—a reminder of the night Nashville trembled "to the earth's centre."

Partying in Nashville in 1827

Dinner at the Hermitage was something to write home about—even for the blue bloods of South Carolina—in 1827, the year before Gen. Andrew Jackson was elected president.

Young Juliana Conner of Charleston, on a wedding trip through the wilds of Tennessee, wrote a glowing account of a late summer night in the home of the man who had been a national hero since the War of 1812.

It was Monday, September 3, 1827, and she and her husband, wealthy plantation owner Henry Workman Conner of Mecklenburg County, North Carolina, had been in Nashville since the Thursday before—at the end of a bone-joggling, fearsome seventeen-day journey by stagecoach over the mountains of East Tennessee.

But on Thursday afternoon, August 30, their horses drew up in front of the most fashionable hotel in town, the Nashville Inn—a great sprawling establishment on the north side of the Public Square, near the river. There they reveled in luxury—in warm baths and rooms "handsomely and fashionably furnished," in elegant parlors where Juliana played the piano while a summer rain beat against the lace-curtained windows.

The "best people" in Nashville—the Foggs, the Catrons, the McGavocks, the McLaughlins, General Jackson, Gov. Sam Houston, Dr. John Shelby—swamped them with invitations to tea, to dinner, to balls, to church, to the theater.

For Juliana and Henry Conner were people of means and important connections.

And nobody had a more appreciative eye for proper manners, for elegant dinners handsomely served, for households tastefully furnished and run than Juliana.

Her first view of the great General Jackson and his much-maligned Rachel, just at dusk on a September day in 1827, is memorable.

She and her husband had ridden the twelve miles out to the Hermitage "in a barouche, servants mounted," she wrote in her diary.

"We arrived before dark, rode up a long avenue and on alighting were met at the hall door by Col. Ogden [Francis B. Ogden, famous engineer-inventor-diplomat who had served as aide-de-camp under Jackson].

"The General and Lady were in the act of descending the stairs. We, of course, remained until they reached the hall and were then presented.

"He is a very venerable, dignified, fine looking man, perfectly easy in manner, but more of that anon.

"Mrs. Jackson received us with equal politeness, led me into a drawing room, insisted upon my taking of some refreshments which were handed, and one would have supposed from the kindness of her manner that she was an old acquaintance.

"After I was rested, she proposed walking into the garden, which is very large and quite her hobby. I never saw any one more enthusiastically fond of flowers.

"She culled for me the only rose which was in bloom and made up a pretty nosegay, and after an agreeable stroll we returned to the drawing room and were joined by several of the gentlemen (for they have always more or less company) and the conversation was kept up, with spirit, until supper was announced."

General Jackson escorted Juliana into the dining room and seated her at Mrs. Jackson's left.

"He occupied the right opposite to me," Juliana wrote. "He pronounced with much solemnity of manner a short grace and then performed the honors of the table, with an attentive politeness which usually characterizes a gentleman."

So, Juliana saw, here was no backwoods hero. Here no snuff-dipping countrywoman.

"Everything was neat and elegant, and complete service of French china, rich cut glass, damask napkins, etc." Juliana wrote.

"After supper, Mrs. Jackson, Maj. Eaton [John H. Eaton, then U.S. senator and later secretary of war, who stirred up a national controversy by his marriage to Peggy O'Neale] and myself formed quite a social trio until we retired.

"Mrs. Jackson accompanied me to the chamber, remained a short time and then bade a 'Good Night'."

The Conners spent the next day at the Hermitage, and Juliana took in every detail of the house from the "splendid French paper" on the walls of the entrance hall to the "rich hangings, carpets, etc. of the two drawing rooms."

On that Tuesday morning, General Jackson escorted Juliana and her husband on a tour of the drawing rooms to show them the portraits of famous men there and to tell them about the mementos "from every part of the Union" given him after the defeat of the British at the Battle of New Orleans in 1815.

The sword presented by the city of New Orleans was "the most splendid piece of workmanship of the time I ever saw," Juliana wrote.

But the things dearest to Jackson were grouped on the mantel. There were the "pistols which were presented to Gen. Washington by Gen. LaFayette, used by the former during his life and were presented by his relative, Mr. Custis, to Gen. Jackson.

"They are preserved with almost sacred veneration and appear to be more highly prized by the owner than all beside, excepting a small pocket spy glass which was used by Gen. Washington during the whole of his military career. These precious reliques are placed together."

Juliana was thrilled when she saw "a rich elegant silver urn" that had been presented Jackson by the "Ladies of South Carolina."

Mornings at the Hermitage were filled with political callers for the General and games for the guests. Juliana was charmed with the way Jackson—sixty years old and straight as an arrow—divided his time between the two.

"I was seated at a small stand playing chess with Col. Ogden," Juliana wrote of that September morn. "The General stood at my side and being an excellent player, he frequently directed my moves, apparently much interested in the fate of the game, and when called off always returned to learn my success.

"There was no trace of the 'military chieftain', as he was called, or other commander. You saw him only a polished gentleman dispensing the most liberal hospitality to all around him."

Before the morning was over, Mrs. Eaton, mother of Major Eaton, arrived to join the party. She, along with "several other ladies, besides a number of gentlemen, was a great addition to the party," Juliana said.

"We sat down to a sumptuous and excellent dinner, about 20 in number. The Gen. saw all his guests arranged and then seated himself at the foot.

"Before leaving the table, the Gen. proposed that the ladies would all join him in drinking to the toast of 'Absent Friends'."

Juliana, who had just received a letter from home about serious illness there, was almost in tears.

"Had my head permitted, I could have drank a bumper

to such a toast," she wrote, "but the sentiment was deeply felt and before me passed in quick review the forms of my loved 'absent friends'."

Young Mr. and Mrs. Conner had to get back to Nashville that night—they were leaving for West Tennessee (for a business trip to Jackson, Tennessee) the next day.

General Jackson offered to write letters of introduction to his friends in Jackson, and have them sent to Conner before he left the Inn the next morning. They would all visit again when the Conners returned to Nashville.

"Mrs. Jackson would not permit me to go without a bouquet which she arranged very tastily, then took of us a most friendly conge and the General drew my arm through his and conducted me to the carriage," Juliana wrote.

The road to West Tennessee was full of horrors as bad as the ones over the mountains from North Carolina had been. Once on the way to Nashville, in a long climb up the mountainside near Asheville, North Carolina, one of the horses pulling their stagecoach had collapsed in the August heat and died in an agonizing fit.

Once the road between Knoxville and Nashville descended at such a sharp angle that the Conners were afraid to stay in the carriage. They got out to walk down the steep slope and could hardly make it without falling.

But the trip through the sparsely settled wilderness of West Tennessee was a nightmare of filthy cabins to sleep in and sickening meals of fatback and greasy cornbread. Only in Jackson, a town just celebrating its fifth anniversary, did they find cultivated people.

When they returned to Nashville two weeks later, on Friday, September 21, the city looked more wonderful than ever to Juliana.

Sam Houston, dashing bachelor hero, had just arrived in town for his inauguration as governor of Tennessee, and was living at the Nashville Inn, where the Conners were staying.

Though Jackson was being talked about everywhere as candidate for president, Mrs. Conner said Houston was "the most popular man in the state.

"His rapid and almost unparalleled rise is sufficient evidence of the fact," Juliana wrote. "He is said to be a very elegant man in his appearance.

"Not yet 38, he enlisted in Jackson's army at 17 as a common soldier, was promoted in regular graduation, then studied to practice law, was made Maj. Gen. of the State, member of Congress and governor—all in less than 20 years.

"He called to pay me a visit as soon as he heard of our arrival—but I had retired. Mr. Conner had been acquainted with him some years since and they met as old acquaintances."

The next day, Saturday, September 22—"a clear, cool morning exhilarating to the feelings"—Juliana beheld the heroic Houston for the first time.

She had just had a visit from Mrs. Henry Rutledge and her daughter, Mrs. Francis Fogg, wives of leading Nashville citizens.

"They had just left when the Governor was announced," Juliana wrote. "Highly raised expectations are usually disappointed, and such Alas! were mine.

"He entered, and I beheld not the godlike grace I have been led to expect, but a figure of Herculean proportions and not possessing, according to my ideas, that elegance or ease for which he is so far famed, but I must and will suspend my opinion until a more intimate knowledge would justify one."

The following Monday, Houston called again.

"I was more pleased with his person and manners which are certainly agreeable," Juliana wrote. "But yet could not discern that superiority of either which has gained him such universal popularity. . . . He does not possess talents of the highest order.

"Of course merely in a visit or two I could not possibly form an opinion of his mind or acquirements. The occasion did not call for a display of either."

Next time Juliana encountered Houston, it was to dance with him at a wedding—the most fashionable wedding of the season in Nashville.

The bride was the fourteen-year-old daughter of one of Nashville's wealthiest and most influential citizens, Dr. John Shelby (see "Dr. John Shelby's Christmas Present"), and the city's society was in a dither over the elaborate preparations.

Thursday, September 27, was the wedding day, and General and Mrs. Jackson arrived in town early for the festivities.

"Mrs. Jackson arrived in the morning and sent me word that she would call for me," Juliana wrote. "I waited on her and we made our arrangements according."

There never had been such preparations for a wedding in Nashville, everybody told her. Dr. Shelby's East Nashville home was being especially enlarged for the occasion, with new windows and doors cut to help with the flow of 500 guests.

Nashville stores, with "very handsome and fancy articles of late fashion," were decking out the most beautiful young ladies in the city. Even old Judge White, former senator and supreme court justice, was in town for the event, and came to the Inn to call on the Conners.

Juliana wrote that Judge White was "a man universally allowed to possess the greatest talents in the state," but his appearance was wizened and quaint.

"He is of the most diminutive size, with apparently scarcely flesh enough to cover his frame," she wrote. "Wears his hair in the Methodist style, hanging down his neck—and is altogether a plain looking old man.

"He has an eye which redeems all—large, clear, blue, with an expression that reaches deep and beams with the intellect. His conversation is nothing remarkable for beauty or style or language, yet from its plain old-fashioned good sense, you cannot but derive pleasure."

Mrs. Jackson came by for Juliana "at an early hour" for the drive to Dr. Shelby's, and they were "ushered into a drawing room filled with ladies."

The bride was "really quite pretty," the Charleston belle wrote. "The groom (a Mr. George Washington Barrows) was a good looking young man—extremely tall, forming a strong contrast to his little wife. The form was Presbyterian, very short, but I presume sufficiently lengthy to be agreeable to the parties. . . .

"After receiving the usual congratulations, the bride and attendants left the room and the married ladies were then requested to adjourn to another room where there was a supper table spread in a most elegant and tasty style, abounding with all the luxuries which could be procured. It was really something quite splendid—far exceeding my expectations."

After dining, the ladies left the table for other guests and proceeded to the ballroom—"a fashionable squeeze unprecedented.

" 'Twas a brilliant scene—the ladies very elegantly dressed, all wearing the semblance of joy," Juliana wrote.

"The General was decidedly the most gallant and courtly man present. . . . His first question to me as I entered was, 'Do you dance?'

"He requested to be allowed to select a partner for me and immediately brought up and introduced the Speaker of the House of Representatives, Dr. Camp, with whom of course I danced—a most colossal figure. We certainly presented a singular contrast.

"My next partner was Governor Houston, who is certainly a most graceful man. Yet I cannot agree with the general opinion relative to his beauty. At least he does not possess the requisites to constitute him such in my opinion; but he has a manner extremely polite and attentive, which cannot fail to render him popular."

The next day began, for Juliana, with a round of visitors, including Mrs. Jackson, and that night she went to the theater.

On the Saturday morning after the wedding, Jackson came by the Inn to see them again, and Juliana was captivated. There were many portraits of him in Nashville, but none caught his animation.

"The oftener I see him, the more I am pleased," she wrote. "I have never seen him on any great occasion, yet cannot but be impressed with the belief of his greatness. . . ."

When Jackson learned that they were to leave Nashville the next morning, he said he would drive in from the Hermitage to see them off and "give us his parting blessing.

"There was a fatherly kindness in his manner which touched the feelings," Juliana wrote.

That afternoon she took tea with Mrs. Rutledge (a native of Charleston who lived in an imposing home in South Nashville) and heard her daughter, Mrs. Fogg, play and sing "in a superior style . . . the soft and plaintive music of Rossini."

Bright and early Sunday morning, September 30, General Jackson was at the Inn to tell the Conners good-bye. He had not waited for Mrs. Jackson because he was afraid that would make him miss seeing the Conners. But, if they could stop, she would meet them along the way.

Then other warmhearted Nashvillians rushed in to say their good-byes. There was Supreme Court Judge Catron's wife. And then Governor Houston, who would be inaugurated next day.

Finally the Conners swung their carriage around the Courthouse Square and past the stores, past the neat rows of tall brick town houses, each behind a low iron fence and a carefully kept green lawn.

They drove past the college buildings—the University of Nashville—on what is now Second Avenue, S., and on past "very beautiful country homes in the environs" farther out, among the rolling hills.

They stopped at the McLemons' home (did she mean McLemore?) before they turned toward Murfreesboro and the Carolinas again.

"We found the General and Mrs. Jackson waiting to receive us at the McLemon's," Juliana wrote. "Took a hearty but affectionate adieu and then left the city. . . .

"We had enjoyed ourselves more than we could have anticipated, had received considerable attention, formed many pleasant acquaintances, and last but not least, had the gratification of enjoying much of the society of General Jackson and lady."

Juliana's impressions, recorded for her own amusement, are now a prized possession of the University of North Carolina.

Nothing she packed in her trunk for the bumpy ride home compared in value with the sparkling view of Nashville, 1827, that people would still be reading more than 150 years later.

William Strickland,
Capitol Architect

William Strickland, honored in 1979 with a fifteen-cent stamp as one of the great architects in American history, is buried in the walls of Tennessee's state capitol, his final work.

But the north winds that whistle past that towering tomb on downtown Nashville's highest hill tell nothing of the fury of the man who spent his last energy battling Tennesseans to make the building noble.

Hindered by penny-pinching legislators who doled out appropriations in two-year driblets, who forced him to use unskilled prison labor to cut down on costs, who failed to recognize the difference between art and mere shelter, Strickland supervised every step of the construction through nine years of rain and heat and galling disagreement.

A handsome, headstrong, and highly gifted man who had known triumph and disappointment, fifty-five-year-old Strickland was already distinguished as both engineer and architect when he arrived in Nashville in 1845. The impressive government buildings, churches, university halls, and other public buildings he had designed for Philadelphia had made it a "city of marble" long before he came to Nashville.

In a sense, Strickland in Nashville was battling a place just emerging from a pioneer town where log houses were still being built to a thriving young city where wealthy merchants and manufacturers were erecting great brick mansions.

Almost symbolically, Andrew Jackson, hero of the frontier, died less than a month after Strickland arrived in Nashville to begin work on the capitol. The fact that Tennessee —already forty-nine years old—was just getting around to building her first capitol told something of the state's slow maturing.

But the precise Strickland, known for his accurate estimates of money and time required to finish a building, was furious when the project he had estimated would take three years dragged on for nine.

As a student of the famed architect Benjamin H. Latrobe, Strickland had made working sketches used in rebuilding the Capitol in Washington after it was burned by the British in the War of 1812. Since boyhood, he had worked with the great masters in the business.

Strickland's father, John Strickland, had been in charge of carpentry on some of Latrobe's finest buildings in Philadelphia. As John Strickland worked on Latrobe's Bank of Philadelphia, the carpenter's ten-year-old son, William, played about the building. His quick mind and his drawing ability caught Latrobe's attention, and in 1803, at age fourteen, William Strickland was apprenticed to Latrobe to learn engineering and architecture.

But young Strickland, for all his charm and excellent work, was independent, sometimes undependable, and "spoiled by his mother," Latrobe said. The impetuous boy, born in Navesink, New Jersey, in November, 1788, would take unauthorized vacations, and in 1805 Latrobe, who had loved him like a son, dismissed him.

After two years of working at painting scenery in New York theaters, young Strickland returned to Philadelphia, making sketches of the local scene. In 1808, when he was not yet twenty-one, Strickland made his "first important and independent architectural drawings" for the Masonic Hall in Philadelphia, according to Agnes A. Gilchrist in her book *William Strickland, Architect and Engineer, 1788-1854.*

At the same time, Strickland's landscapes were being shown in two Philadelphia art museums, the Pennsylvania Academy of Fine Arts and the Columbia Society of Artists. Strickland, a member of both societies, served as director of the former until he moved to Nashville.

A favorite in Philadelphia society, Strickland was involved in everything from philosophy to geology, from canal and railroad design to comparative religion, and he was particularly fond of fine music, good food, and sparkling conversation.

He was a member of the Episcopal Church, and when he married pretty Rachel M. Trenchard in 1812, "near his 24th birthday," the ceremony was at Christ Episcopal Church in Philadelphia. Eventually Strickland and his wife had six children, and in his days of success he and his wife and two daughters traveled for nearly a year in Europe.

With remarkable versatility, he worked at everything from map-making and surveying to painting portraits and illustrating books. During the War of 1812 he was commissioned to survey Philadelphia with an eye to the possible approaches of the enemy, and he was instructed to design defenses for the city.

But by the end of the war, he was occupied full time as an architect, designing Philadelphia churches and buildings at the University of Pennsylvania medical school. Always conservative in materials and in methods of construction, he used iron for structural strength and made liberal use of marble to prevent fire. He was one of the first to use central heating and indoor toilets, and his combination of solid construction and pleasing design made him the unofficial architect of Philadelphia.

In competition with other distinguished architects, including his old teacher Latrobe, Strickland won the commission to build the Second Bank of the United States. (Latrobe's design came in second.)

That building, called "one of the finest buildings designed and built in this country," borrowed heavily from the Parthenon in Athens, and its columned porticoes, along with the practical and comfortable design of the interior, helped establish Strickland as one of the nation's top architects.

During the six years he supervised the construction of that building, Strickland worked on at least eighteen other important buildings, including churches, a theater, and a courthouse. At the same time, he did the engineering work showing possible routes for the Delaware and Chesapeake Canal.

At that time, when American cities were torn between building railroads and canals, Strickland became an expert at both. He spent little time at designing residences.

But he always found time for civic and social activities, and he had a leading role in entertaining Lafayette when he visited Philadelphia in 1824. He even wrote a song in honor of the French hero and was a director of the Musical Fund Society in Philadelphia until he came to Nashville.

A gregarious soul, he enjoyed the feasts of the Beefsteak Club, and he was outstanding enough in his intellectual pursuits to be elected to the American Philosophical Society in Philadelphia.

In 1825, the year after he helped entertain Lafayette, Strickland was in England for eight months, and he had a marvelous time as he carried out his commission there: to obtain, for a group of Philadelphia citizens, top advice on whether the city's commerce would be better served by building railroads or canals.

England, with her advanced experience in both, was so full of constructive ideas that Strickland came home to publish his findings in a book titled *Reports on Canals, Railroads and Roads.*

In 1826, thirty-eight-year-old Strickland moved briefly to Harrisburg while he worked for the state of Pennsylvania to survey part of the railroad and canal system linking Philadelphia to Pittsburgh.

But Strickland resigned that position to work on a number of important architectural commissions that suddenly came his way. Much of this work survives today, including the Delaware Breakwater that he built off Lewes, Delaware, to protect the harbor for ships sailing in to Philadelphia.

Among his innovative designs of that period in Philadelphia is the Naval Home for retired seamen, designed in 1826. In 1828, when the old steeple of Independence Hall had to be restored, it was Strickland who designed a new steeple and supervised the construction.

In rapid succession, Strickland designed the United States Mint and St. Paul's Episcopal Church in Philadelphia. In 1832, when he was forty-four, he designed the building now recognized as the most original of his designs: the Philadelphia Exchange. It is that triangular building that is shown on the new fifteen-cent Strickland stamp, and the structure still stands between three streets, with rows of columns on three sides.

Strickland gained special grace for the building when he rounded the apex of the triangle into a semicircle and placed a tower above the rounded portico. The tower, or cupola, a bold departure from the usual dome, was designed thirteen years before Strickland used a similar tower to rise eighty feet above the Tennessee capitol. Both were modeled after the choragic monument of Lysicrates in Athens.

The tower above the Philadelphia Exchange (a merchant's exchange) was a first in the architectural world. Latrobe and Thomas Jefferson had discussed it, but never used it. Strickland, who must have felt a particular pride in it, had an office there until he moved to Nashville in 1845.

A warmhearted, generous man who inspired both his students and the workmen who constructed his buildings, Strickland attracted top artisans of the country to work on his buildings. When the Philadelphia Exchange was completed, he offered them a toast at a banquet given in their honor. When one of the stonemasons working on the Tennessee capitol was killed in an accident on the job, the grieving Strickland designed the monument.

In 1838, while he was touring Europe with his wife and two daughters, Strickland made lasting friendships among outstanding Englishmen in his profession and was invited to witness the coronation of Queen Victoria.

London investors interested in developing the land in the triangle where the Ohio and the Mississippi rivers flow together, at Cairo, Illinois, formed the Cairo City and Canal Company and commissioned Strickland to draw up plans for building sea walls that would make the area floodproof.

But in 1840, before Strickland could complete his survey of the area, a devastating flood wiped out those buildings already there. The result was failure of the company and abandonment of the plan.

At the same time, Strickland was helping edit a book published in London in 1841 on *Public Works in the United States* and he was elected to the Royal Institution of Civil Engineers in 1842.

But by that time the financial panic that had begun in 1837 had so cut off building funds that Strickland found himself without work, and he turned to Washington for commissions on various government buildings between 1842 and 1844.

He was well known there, having worked as consultant on the U.S. Capitol with distinguished architects Latrobe and Charles Bulfinch. It was while he was in Washington that he received the fateful letter inviting him to submit plans for Tennessee's capitol.

No evidence today shows precisely how the building commission in Nashville knew about Strickland and his distinguished work. Certainly there were Nashville merchants and bankers, as well as government officials, who made frequent business trips to Philadelphia and would have seen the handsome buildings he had designed there.

William Nichol, president of the Bank of Tennessee and chairman of the Board of Capitol Commissioners, had advanced $30,000 to buy Cedar Knob as the site of the state's capitol. He must have seen Strickland's work during his visits to Philadelphia, and he must have been pleased when the Board, meeting on June 16, 1844, authorized him to write Strickland and ask him to submit plans for Tennessee's "State House."

The state would pay Strickland $500 for his plans and $2,500 per year if he would move to Nashville and supervise construction of the building. Moreover, they would pay his travel expenses if he wanted to look the site over.

But it was nearly a year later, on April 2, 1845, that the Board wrote Strickland to urge him to come to Nashville as soon as possible to begin work on the capitol. Over a month later, after a strenuous trip by train, steamboat, and stagecoach, Strickland arrived in Nashville to turn the rocky hill towering over the town into a pedestal for the building that was to cap his career.

Strickland's Triumph
in Marble and Bronze

When Philadelphia architect William Strickland stepped out of a stagecoach at the Nashville Inn on May 22, 1845, there was no hint of the trials that would stalk him to his death here.

No hint of the agony that would stretch a three-year task into nine years of fighting for funds to pay for the next step. No hint of backwoods legislators who wanted to polish off the building job with a coat of whitewash and a sturdy board fence around the whole.

For Strickland—elegant architect-engineer whose designs were sought for important buildings in many cities in this country—had dealt only with the more enlightened members of the Tennessee citizenry. They had considered several architects before they enthusiastically approved his plans.

Strickland, a favorite in Philadelphia social and intellectual circles and father of four living children, had told his wife Rachel that he would be back home in Philadelphia in three years, when the Tennessee capitol was finished. It was years before she gave up on that promise and joined him in Nashville.

It was galling to fifty-five-year-old Strickland, known in his profession as a man exact in his calculations of expected costs and date of completion of a building, to see the project delayed by everything from the inefficiency of prison labor to the costly task of excavating for the foundations atop what had been Cedar Knob.

But he had the enthusiastic backing of the Board of Commissioners, appointed by the Tennessee legislature to keep close watch on the construction of the capitol—the first the forty-nine-year-old state had ever built.

After all, Tennessee had switched its headquarters frequently, with the legislature meeting in Knoxville from 1796 to 1812 (with the exception of one day, September 21, 1807, in Kingston); in Nashville from 1812 to 1817; in Murfreesboro from 1818 to 1823; and in Nashville again from 1824 to the present. The legislature did not make the final decision on Nashville as permanent capital until 1843, and it was then that a commission was set up to make plans for building a state capitol.

Meantime, from 1824 until the capitol was ready for occupancy in 1853, the legislature met in Nashville's Masonic Hall, on the north side of Church Street, between Fourth and Fifth avenues. From that two-story building standing near the site of the present Third National Bank, legislators fumed impatiently for years while they doled out a total of $900,500 for completion of the lofty stone capitol on the city's highest hill.

Immediately after his arrival in Nashville, fast-working Strickland surveyed the situation—the steep hill formerly called Cedar Knob where workmen had already cleared the thick growth of cedar trees, and the quarry hardly one mile to the west, where stone for the building would be excavated. (That quarry, according to maps furnished recently by Robert Webster of the Metro Planning Commission, covered an area that is now the site of the Henry Hale Housing Project, plus a small area somewhat east of it. The quarry lay between Twelfth and Fourteenth avenues and was bordered by Jo Johnston and Charlotte.)

To haul the huge blocks of limestone—some of them weighing ten tons each—to the top of Capitol Hill, Strickland designed a road from the quarry to circle the hill. That involved building a bridge across a small creek.

The Board of Commissioners told Strickland that he would have to use prison labor for the quarrying (to save about $100,000 in labor costs) and both he and other workmen on the job resented that requirement. Without prison labor, Strickland estimated, total cost of the building would be about $340,000. With prisoners doing some of the rougher work, the cost might be cut to $210,000.

On June 18, 1845, Strickland signed the contract to supervise the construction of the capitol he had designed, and he was soon hiring hundreds of stonecutters, stone carvers, "men rubbing stone," "men quarrying, turning and rolling stone for cutters," stone setters, stonemasons, bricklayers, carpenters and wood-carvers for the fine hand-carved doors and cabinets, ironworkers, plumbers, road builders, foremen for the various jobs, and night watchmen.

The men worked for as little as $1 a day or as much as $2.50 per day—depending on the skill required. Highly skilled artisans who had worked on multimillion-dollar capitols in other states flocked to Nashville to work on the Tennessee capitol. Men originally from Ireland, Germany, England, and Wales put their best efforts into the building that Strickland designed as fireproof in structure and noble in line.

He made it of solid stone, with foundations 7 feet thick and all other exterior walls 4½ feet thick. It was to be one of the rare buildings with polished (or rubbed) stone both inside and out.

Strickland made detailed models of the capitol and its eighty-foot tower to show the Building Commission, and word of its elegance soon spread throughout Nashville, a town of 7,000 that had been accustomed to pomp and circumstance during the years of Andrew Jackson's military fame and his presidency.

Elaborate parades and ceremony were the bread and meat of the town's social life in those preradio, premovie, pretelevision days, and only a few weeks after Strickland arrived, citizens from all over the state turned out for public meetings and the funeral parade to mourn the death of Jackson on June 8, 1845.

Less than a month later, on July 4, the citizens—from servants to governor—would pack Capitol Hill to see the cornerstone of the great marble capitol laid. Strickland, in his bed at the Nashville Inn that sunny morning, was delighted to wake to the sound of crowds finding their place in the parade to Capitol Hill.

"That smiling morn which ushered in the day of jubilee," Strickland wrote, set a happy mood for his vast undertaking. Various city and state "societies, denominations, or fraternities" were scheduled to march from the Public Square and up the dusty street to the hilltop for the grand ceremony, and at 11:15 A.M. the town bell was rung to signal the start of the parade.

In colorful uniforms, foot soldiers and mounted troops marched to the roll of drums and martial music, and crowds along the way cheered the Nashville Blues and the Harrison Guards, the governor, the capitol commissioners, the architect, and the orator of the day.

"The whole hill was covered with one dense mass of human beings" as the Freemasons "made a majestically imposing appearance" in the procession, proud of the fact that both architect Strickland and Wilkins Tannehill, outstanding Mason, had leading parts in the ceremony that day.

The Reverend J. Thomas Wheat, rector of Christ Episcopal Church and chaplain of the Grand Lodge, opened the program with a prayer. Ladies shaded by parasols and—if they were lucky—seated in their carriages listened intently as Edwin H. Ewing, chief speaker of the day, "argued most irresistably in favor of the erection of a State House which would do honor to the high character of the State."

Men, women, and children joined in the applause, and then there was a hush as the climax of the day came: "mementoes of a past era" were placed in the cornerstone, and Strickland presented the plumb, square, and level to Tannehill, as Master Mason, to seal the stone.

Tannehill closed the ceremonies with his salute to Strickland, predicting that "the people will behold an edifice arise which will be honorable to the State, and an enduring monument to your well earned reputation as an architect."

To supervise the whole undertaking, Strickland had a tiny frame office built on the hill, where he could take shelter from winter winds and blazing sun. Total cost of the office, including a porch for $10 and plastering for $8.50, was $68.50, Strickland noted with his usual precision.

The quarry supplying stone for the capitol had been selected in January, 1845, before Strickland arrived. Members of the Board of the Capitol Commission, along with the superintendent of the state prison, made the decision. They chose a quarry (owned by Samuel Watkins) less than a mile from Capitol Hill because it was close to the prison, then on Church Street, between Fifteenth and Sixteenth avenues. That made it convenient for prison labor.

Five months after the cornerstone was laid, Strickland had "all the rough masonry, and most of the cut work of the crypt or cellar story" finished, he reported. He had designed arched ceilings for the halls and most of the rooms, and in the winter, when it was too cold for outdoor construction, he had 150 stonecutters, in addition to prison labor, cutting stones for the first floor and its groined arches, or preparing stone for the piers and columns that would be lifted to their high pedestals in the spring. Much of the quarried stone was hauled inside the prison yard where prisoners could do the rough stonework.

Much of Strickland's time was taken in hiring new workmen, instructing laborers on new methods of handling tremendous ropes and spars to lift ten-ton blocks of stone in place on the rising walls and the tower that ran from the foundation of the building to a point eighty feet above the roof.

The tower, an innovation on Greek Revival buildings when he first used it, was part of his design for the capitol from the beginning. He had used a similar tower thirteen years earlier on one of his best-known buildings—the Philadelphia Exchange—but Tennesseans through the years have entertained themselves with stories about its being an "afterthought."

Strickland designed the capitol to be heated by central heat (with hot-air flues built into the walls), as he had done in his Philadelphia buildings. He designed indoor plumbing for the capitol, with water closets for the toilets supplied by rainwater drained from the roof to storage tanks under the terrace.

For the House of Representatives, on the second floor, he designed an enormous chandelier with handsome bronze symbols of Tennessee—Indians, buffalo, corn, and tobacco. That bronze chandelier, hanging from the forty-two-foot ceiling, so awed backwoods legislators years later that they—fearing its weight over their heads—had it removed.

To insure against fire, Strickland had practically the entire building made of stone and iron. The rafters, made of iron at Cumberland Iron Works, weighed 210 tons and cost $15,700.

The copper roof, made in Pittsburgh and shipped to Nashville by boat in 1851, weighed 27½ tons and cost $12,267. The massive fluted columns on the exterior of the building—eight each on the north and south, and six each on the east and west—were hand-carved, and the exquisite work on the Ionic capitals crowning the columns became one of the handsomest features of the building.

The entire capitol, covering three-quarters of an acre and reaching four stories, to a height of over 206 feet, was designed to lift the spirit with its lofty, vaulted corridors; its regal hall niches for busts of Tennessee heroes; its sixteen columns, over twenty-one feet tall, each made from one piece of marble, to border the balcony in the House of Representatives; its twelve columns of red marble from East Tennessee that support the balcony of the Senate; its massive double stairway of marble that rises, freestanding, from the first floor to the main floor, where the legislature meets.

As Strickland was delayed by cholera epidemics that struck some of the workmen, by tardy appropriations, and by ignorant legislators, his workers were inspired by his insistence on top-quality material and workmanship. No detail of the building was too small for his attention. Workers knew that they owed their safety in handling the tremendous stone blocks and columns to his engineering skill. His sense of humor, his generosity, and his quick mind kept the men working through numerous difficulties.

Samuel D. Morgan, only commissioner on the Capitol Board from the beginning of the project till the end, was an invaluable go-between in the sometimes bitter tiffs between Strickland and the legislators. One legislator, enraged at the thought of another $200,000 appropriation, suggested that it be reduced to $10,000 "to complete the building, whitewash it thoroughly, and put a substantial fence around it."

Strickland—out of patience—called the legislators "nimcompoops" and fought almost to the end of his life for five years' pay for his son Francis, who worked as his assistant.

Finally Strickland, who had been a favorite guest at fashionable parties, weddings, and holiday festivities in Nashville, lost patience with "people of mediocre intellect who depended on their money" for their position in society, according to Mrs. Nell Savage Mahoney in an article about Strickland in the March, 1950, *Tennessee Historical Quarterly.*

The capitol was far from finished when the legislature met there for the first time, on Monday, October 3, 1853, but their praise for the "magnificent Capitol" filled the marble halls for a few shining days. Then the polished marble halls and floors, not yet softened with draperies or carpeting, presented problems in acoustics, and soon Strickland was swamped with criticism.

On January 1, 1854, Strickland asked the legislators again for back pay for his son, and three months later he was dead. Morgan said Strickland's health had failed as he became "intemperate," but the men who worked with him said his efficiency never failed.

On the day before he died, sixty-six-year-old Strickland stumbled and fell on the post office steps. On Thursday, April 6, 1854, at 4 A.M., he died in his room at the City Hotel.

Six weeks before he died, the legislature had voted to permit Strickland to be buried in the walls of the capitol he had designed, "in honor of his genius in erecting so grand a work."

The legislature paid Strickland's widow the $146.61 they owed him, and they paid his funeral expenses of $108 (including $90 for "a burial case" and $18 for "a winding sheet"). And for two years they engaged Strickland's son, Francis, to supervise completion of the building.

But on Saturday morning, April 8, 1854, funeral services for William Strickland were held in the House of Representatives and the building was packed with mourners. "Two or three thousand" people pushed inside the building he had designed, and later they packed the north slope of Capitol Hill as he was entombed within the capitol walls.

Other buildings still standing in Nashville were designed by Strickland (including Downtown Presbyterian and St. Mary's Catholic Church) and others long gone were his work. But even unlettered Andrew Johnson, governor at the time of Strickland's death, was awed at the rare "temple of government."

"Let us go . . . to your State Capitol and look at the magnificence of that building," he wrote. "As we contemplate the work, the mind naturally suggests the inquiry: What hand constructed? Who built this house?—and we are filled with admiration of the mind that planned, and the men of labor that raised up this beautiful temple of the State. Are not these men of some importance to the Country?"

When Cholera Laid
Our City Low

One "stout laboring man" in Nashville felt perfectly well as he ate his lunch of cabbage and potatoes on June 4, 1873. But by midafternoon he was stricken with the ghastly illness that people had been whispering about. By sundown he was dead.

"Up to this time I had doubts about cholera having our fair city in its grasp," Dr. W. K. Bowling, a prominent physician of the time, wrote of that death. "I doubted no longer. This man died of cholera."

The swiftness of its attack, the helplessness of both patient and doctor to do anything about it, the mystery of where the disease came from and what caused it made cholera the terror of the nineteenth century.

Patients were so stunned by the violence of the attack that they seemed to lose all interest in living. One man said he had no warning at all until he "pitched forward in the street, as if knocked down with an axe."

Half the people stricken with cholera died. Doctors made frantic jabs at easing the patients' suffering, but nothing "cured" the disease.

When cholera struck, it was like "turning on a faucet and letting all the fluids rush out of the body," one doctor explained. The patient's skin turned blue and clammy, and sank in shriveled, puckered folds. When he died, his body was "dry as parchment."

The desperate effort to prevent cholera's spread was the

beginning of much of the state public-health work and sanitation systems in Nashville and other stricken cities throughout the world.

Five times in the forty years before 1873 cholera had swept over the United States and left hundreds dead in Nashville, worst-hit city in the state.

For weeks before the "stout laboring man" died, there had been suspicious deaths in Nashville. Not only was the general public alarmed; doctors whispered to each other of "strange cases" they were seeing.

"Suddenly in the last week of May, physicians would stop each other on the street and inquire, with long visages, 'Anything suspicious in your practice?' " Dr. Bowling reported.

None of them, remembering the 659 lives wiped out in a brief epidemic in Nashville seven years before, wanted to admit what they all feared.

For one thing, Nashville was in the midst of a big trade fair, with thousands of visitors in the city. The cholera scare would ruin everything.

"The city was crowded to suffocation, and the trains from everywhere to everywhere burdened with human beings, coming to or going from the show," Dr. Bowling recalled.

"All public places were flooded with gas light and animated with the music . . . of Italia's black-eyed daughters, thronging the streets with violins and harps.

"The Opera House, long silent as an oyster, was lighted up in her holiday habiliments. Nashville was looking up."

Tennessee's capitol city, with a population suddenly grown to 26,000, was crowing about her fifth bank and two new daily papers. A new subdivision, "Jones' Addition," would be opened soon, and corner lots would "go like hot cakes."

"When boom!" the doctor said. "The epidemic struck as suddenly as the volcano on Pompeii."

Actually in that last week of May, 1873, there had been mysterious deaths that other doctors were already labeling cholera: the Negro washwoman who fell ill at 2 P.M. and was dead two hours later; the four other people in the neighborhood who died the same way at about the same time.

"On June 1, a little white girl who stayed at a fruit stand near the post office, in the center of the city, sickened with diarrhea, went to her boarding house on Union Street between Summer and High, and died in a few hours," Dr. Bowling said.

There were others, falling ill in rapidly mounting numbers. Like "Miss H., 11 years old, a fine healthy child, plump and ruddy," who lived on North College Street. She woke up at 6 A.M. one June morning, "in perfect health.

"An hour later she was suddenly struck with diarrhea," the doctor reported. "I saw her 20 minutes later. She was suffering stomach cramps, vomiting, extreme diarrhea. She had no pulse, and her skin was cold and damp. Six hours later she was dead."

The only clue, the bewildered doctor said, was that she "had eaten 12 peanuts the preceding evening."

Then there was "one of the most beautiful and accomplished young ladies in the city, who ate two or three pickles and died."

And even though every doctor in town was convinced that overindulgence—whether eating, drinking, or other excess—hastened death among the stricken, one preacher died after eating "that innocent New England dish, strawberry shortcake."

Some doctors argued that the disease, "like malaria," rose from the earth in poisonous clouds, to settle over low places. Others, like Dr. Bowling, mapped the spots where the disease had struck and decided that "cholera likes high places, hill tops." Like fallout, it "fell from the heavens."

Doctors in other cities had noted that cholera strikes

hardest in filthy areas, and Dr. J. Berrien Lindsley, who helped found the state board of health to combat just such epidemics, called Nashville the "filthiest city on the continent."

Nashville's cellars, blasted out of limestone, were a curse to the city, he said. The open sewage that drained into porous limestone contaminated cellars, cisterns, and springs. He, like many other doctors, looked to the water supply as the source of the disease.

But Dr. Bowling, who taught at the University of Nashville School of Medicine and helped edit the *Nashville Journal of Medicine and Surgery,* was outraged at such a suggestion.

Most Nashvillians, he said, drank from "pure, cold springs," and what could be freer of disease?

And what about the campaign to get sewage underground? Dr. Bowling was horrified. While Paris, France, and other European cities had installed underground sewers as a direct result of earlier cholera epidemics, Dr. Bowling looked upon that as folly.

He argued that in low sections of Nashville, recently flooded, where "every imaginable abomination . . . lies rotting, seething and weltering in unobstructed sun," there had been no cholera.

Sewerage should be aboveground, with the only true disinfectants operating on its cause: "the circumambient air and gorgeous sunshine," he said.

Crawford Street, "between Capitol and McGavock hills," was "the filthiest street in the city," he said, and not a single case of cholera had appeared there.

Meantime, everybody who could flee the rotting city did, and the others died in such number that there were not enough coffins to go around, and not enough gravediggers left for that grim duty.

Dr. Bowling had a favorite theory:

"A man having this cholera germ in him at the same time with vegetables, fruits or animal products, he explodes, the same harmony existing between them as between fire and gun-powder."

He cited "two poor little boys over the river, who went to a plum tree, ate a quantity of the fruit, and were found dead in the path homeward, with signs of cholera about them."

Also there were two little brothers in Edgefield (East Nashville) who ate mulberries from a tree in their father's yard, and died that same day.

"Our janitor, here at the Medical College, took two glasses of buttermilk, and was buried the same evening," Dr. Bowling said.

"Ice cream and strawberries carried off numbers, and snapbeans were as fatal as arsenic. Buttermilk was almost as unerring in its death-aim. Blackberries were a sure shot, but cabbage and potatoes, being more easily procured, were the most fatal."

From June 7, the day Nashville doctors admitted there was cholera in the city, newspapers began publishing daily lists of fatalities. Within a week, twenty-five people a day were dying of cholera. Two days later, forty-four people died.

The worst day in Nashville's cholera history came on Friday, June 20, 1873, when seventy-two persons died of the disease; people spoke of it afterward as "Black Friday."

In that same June, the worst in Nashville's history and the worst in the state for cholera, 750 persons died of the disease. The six cholera epidemics that hit the city took a total of almost 3,000 lives.

Men stricken with the disease in the middle of the street could not make it to the curb. Children in the middle of their rooms could not make it to their beds.

Households were found where every member of the family had died within twenty-four hours—sometimes as many as six people—and there was no one to tell of the tragedy.

In New Bethel, a little Negro community at the edge of the city, on Granny White Road, some two hundred people died, and at least fifty-three of them were hastily buried in a mass grave, without benefit of coffin.

Dr. Bowling, mourning for them in their helplessness, said, "They marched uncomplaining through their gardens to their graves.

"All the talking, the gas-ing and printer's ink, and resolving and meeting and deliberating and burning tar and brimstone on the streets, to kill the cholera gnats, did poor New Bethel no good."

And then he added, most surprisingly:

"It is not for us to seek the cause of cholera!"

Dr. Lindsley could remember the first epidemic that struck Nashville, forty years earlier, in 1833, and the blind terror that followed.

"I well remember, when quite a boy myself, how everybody was scared by the graphic and terrible reports of cholera," Dr. Lindsley wrote in 1875.

"From the filthy tenements of Hindustan in 1817, it had swept across Europe, and finally landed on the western continent in 1832. Russia, Poland and other parts of Europe had suffered terribly.

"It was looked upon as a grand mystery, a fate, perhaps a judgment. By December 14, 1832, the first case in Nashville appeared, but there was no alarm until the middle of January and through February, 1833. June was the worst month, with 70 deaths in Nashville from cholera."

That was when Nashville had a population of 6,000, and all but 500 had fled the city.

Dr. Bowling refused to believe that transmission of the disease came about through "men or the things of men."

But it was obvious that the disease rode the route of

commerce. Out of 50,000 pilgrims of the Mohammedan faith who had journeyed to Mecca in 1831, 20,000 had died there of Asiatic cholera. As the others scattered, they took cholera with them.

Across Europe, the disease sped to Ireland, where the island was quickly infected. Irish citizens crowded onto ships in the nearest port, and many died on board and were buried at sea.

Since they were not allowed to land in New York, the Irish immigrants entered Canada and took riverboats down the St. Lawrence and through the new Erie Canal. When the boats passed through locks, the Irishmen fought New York guards and jumped ashore.

Soon New York City, Philadelphia, and Baltimore were caught in a raging epidemic, and members of ships' crews sailing from there carried cholera to New Orleans. From there it came up the Mississippi to wipe out thousands of inlanders.

On April 19, 1833, the steamboat *Tobacco Plant* arrived at Nashville and reported eight deaths on board—all from cholera. Among the passengers had been one of Nashville's most prominent citizens, Alexander Porter. He had left the stricken ship in West Tennessee, in an effort to escape cholera; but as he traveled overland toward Nashville he was stricken and died at Dresden.

Though cholera often hit hardest among the poor and dirty, it also killed many of the city's wealthiest citizens. Josiah Nichol, "banker, merchant, head of a large family," died soon after Porter. Francis Porterfield, "one of the most enterprising merchants," spent a healthy, happy Sunday. But the next morning he was dead of cholera.

Dr. James Roane (son of Tennessee's second governor), one of the founders of the state medical society and "one of the great names in Tennessee medicine . . . was incessantly busy day and night with patients dangerously ill.

"He was attacked with cholera one morning," Dr. Lindsley wrote. "He died that night at 8 P.M."

All but three of the eighty-eight prisoners at the state penitentiary were stricken, and both doctors and kind citizens labored to attend them.

When that first epidemic hit Europe, in 1832, so many poor people died that they thought it was a plot, a "poison" released by the rich to get rid of them. They rioted in protest until they observed that the rich too fell—some of them stricken on the ballroom floor and dying on their way to the hospital two hours later.

In this country, the epidemic became a moral question, with some ministers preaching that it was God's will. Sometimes physicians, stumped for an answer, agreed with the preachers.

"It comes down upon people like contents of Pandora's box," Dr. Bowling wrote. "It comes not from man to man, but upon him. The disease fell upon the city. The seed cloud spread itself over the city, and sifted its destructive missiles upon its population.

"To appeal to water sources or geological formations for an answer to the puzzle is only ridiculous."

Civic pride entered the argument too. When New York doctors traveled to Nashville to study the disease, they mentioned the city's filth and poverty.

"The poor of New York live more miserably than the slaves in the South," Dr. Bowling countered, and cited sickening evidence from New York medical journals.

Both cities had relied on hogs that roamed the city streets to act as scavengers and clean up the garbage, and had resisted some doctors' advice to pen them up.

One old lady living near Columbia had as sensible an explanation for the spread of cholera as Dr. Bowling did.

"Where Duck River is, cholera ain't," the doctor quoted her. "Where Duck River ain't, cholera is."

As the disease struck, Nashvillians fled to neighboring towns and spread the epidemic.

Pulaski, with a population of 1,000, stopped all business, and all but 200 persons fled the town. Even so, as many as 25 persons died in one week.

Fayetteville and Memphis had their share. In later epidemics, not only riverboats but also railroads spread infected travelers along their routes. Railroad workmen traveling out of Nashville spread the disease to Chattanooga, Birmingham, and all stations between.

President James K. Polk had just returned to Nashville at the end of his term in the White House, in the spring of 1849, when cholera struck the city the second time.

That was sixteen years after the first epidemic, and doctors were loathe to admit its return. But there were thirty-three deaths in Nashville in February, and a sudden increase in May. President Polk, just getting settled in his home at the corner of Seventh and Union, told his wife they had better leave the city before the epidemic got worse.

But it struck him suddenly one Sunday morning and he battled the disease for two weeks. On June 16, the day he was buried at the Old City Cemetery, there were thirty-four other burials there—all deaths from cholera. It was the worst day of the cholera epidemic of 1849.

By August the epidemic had disappeared. (Even today doctors are not sure why they suddenly stop.)

But cholera, a disease known in Asia more than 2,000 years ago, swept this country again in 1850, 1854, 1866, and 1873—each time introduced from foreign ports. By the time the epidemic of 1883 struck Europe (killing 800,000 in Russia alone), a German scientist, Dr. Robert Koch, had tracked down the germ.

In 1876, at one of the high points of medical history—when Pasteur and Lister were revolutionizing medicine with their discovery of germs and ways to combat them—Dr. Koch discovered the cholera germ, a "comma-shaped" bacteria found in the intestines of victims.

Out of his study it became clear that water contaminated by the excreta of cholera victims is the chief means of spreading the disease. Food can be contaminated by flies that come into contact with the excreta. Unwashed hands can be the lethal agent.

There is still no way of "curing" cholera. Once anyone gets it, the only treatment today is to overcome the violent dehydration by introducing gallons of water into the patient by intravenous injection. (No cholera patient, seared as he is by thirst, can swallow water.)

But the disease has not touched this country since 1892, and it was stopped at the doorstep then by strict quarantine.

One of Dr. Koch's students, inspired by the scientist's studies, helped found the Massachusetts Board of Health Laboratories, chiefly for study of water purification and sewage disposal.

As a result of that study, cities throughout this country have patterned their own protective water and sewage systems.

In 1892, when eight foreign ships arrived in New York harbor at about the same time, all heavily laden with cholera patients, the city was prepared. All ships were quarantined, and no epidemic occurred.

"The new science in America completely outwitted the greatest scourge," one medical writer announced in triumph.

The vaccine developed soon after that protects all military men and other travelers to those countries where Asiatic cholera occurs. No one from those regions can enter this country without proof of his vaccination.

Now an international organization set up to protect all

countries from the spread of disease keeps a relentless eye on travelers.

In June, 1964, Dr. R. H. Hutcheson, Tennessee's commissioner of health, received an alarming call from a public-health official in California. A cholera epidemic was raging in Hong Kong, Burma, and the Philippines, and a Tennessee-bound serviceman from that area had, mistakenly, been cleared through the California port of entry without a check on his cholera vaccination.

Dr. Hutcheson telephoned the county health officer in the town where the serviceman was believed to have gone, and the officer sent the sheriff to find him. He did, and the serviceman showed the health officer proof of his vaccination.

"All a case of error in the record keeping in California," Dr. Hutcheson said. "But it shows how we are set up now with a worldwide net to keep cholera out."

The Battle of Nashville

On a bleak, gray December 15, in 1864, captured Nashville woke to the thunder of cannon—the first ominous rumble of death and pain that was to lock the city in horror for two days.

For it was on December 15 and 16 of that year that the grim Battle of Nashville was fought, rolling over hills across the city's southern border, ranging in a wide loop southward from Charlotte Pike on the west to Harding Pike and Hillsboro Pike, Granny White Pike, Franklin Pike, and Nolensville Pike on the east. (The roads were turnpikes then —hence the shortened name, "pike.")

The battlefield, looping in a wide band some twenty miles long, covered thirty-five square miles and some of the highest hills in the area. The two armies struggled almost toe-to-toe and left their torn footprints over more than 22,000 acres of mud, rain, sleet, and blood.

It all ended in crushing defeat for Confederate forces in icy rain and darkness on the second day, and that defeat, many historians believe, spelled doom for the Southern cause.

When one visits those same spots today, scanning the hilltop where courageous men on both sides fell to rifle fire, cannonball and saber blow, the twilight scene is shrouded in heartbreak.

Few traces are left now of the fortifications that both armies built, but there are some buildings still standing that

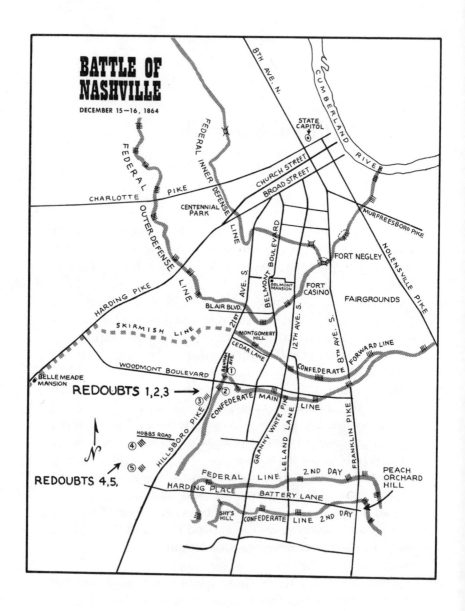

Map by Bob Turner, *The Tennessean*

shook to the roar of battle and still bear the scars of gunfire. And those who climb the hills can still find dim traces of old entrenchments.

On street corners where we meet today, in city church-yards and on lofty suburban drives that give magnificent views of Nashville, men died in 1864 with bullets through their heads and horses shot from under them.

On hillsides where charming homes stand on landscaped lawns today, soldiers slipped and slid in foot-deep mud, and their bare feet trailed blood in the snow as they built their flimsy ramparts.

In bright dining rooms where families sit down to a variety of food, there is the ghostly knowledge that in 1864 thousands of hungry men fought close by, slashing their way across the city's southern border without a bite to eat for twenty-four hours at a time. Parched corn after the battle was the most they could hope for.

Nightmares were all around.

As Nashvillians today follow the battle's progress from the first boom of Union cannon on top of Fort Negley to the last bloody retreat of the Confederate army down Shy's Hill and out Franklin and Granny White pikes, the well-documented stories abound.

One Confederate officer, hurriedly washing up at a stream after a fierce encounter near Hillsboro Road on December 15, felt something sticky in his beard. Horrified, he realized it was part of the brain of a fellow soldier killed hours before as they fought side by side.

Not far away, where Calvary United Methodist Church stands today (at 3701 Hillsboro Road), on a hill just north of Green Hills Shopping Center, men fought desperately and were killed that day. There the highest-ranking Union officer to lose his life in the Battle of Nashville, Col. Sylvester Hill, was shot through the head and died that December 15, in the afternoon.

The trenches so hurriedly dug out by the Confederates before that battle still run down into a V-shape in back of the church today. Children in the church's kindergarten clamber up and down the grassy trenches in play, and it has been years since anyone found a Minié ball there. ("Minié balls" were conical lead bullets fired from rifles.)

But when all of that area south of the city was still farmland, years after the Battle of Nashville, heavy rains used to wash Minié balls and old uniform buckles—both Confederate and Union—down the hillsides and into ditches along Hillsboro Road.

On that first day of battle, thousands of soldiers slapped their legs against their horses or jogged on foot across the broad area running along both sides of what is now Woodmont Boulevard. They were, for the most part, Union soldiers swinging out of the west (from Harding Pike) to meet the Confederates head-on along Hillsboro Pike.

For the Battle of Nashville was one of the best planned of the Civil War. In the first place, the city was said to be the best fortified area in the country.

That in itself told something of the city's importance in the grand scheme of the Union forces—to protect the captured Nashville as a center of supplies for the Union army, and to hold open its railroad and river shipping facilities.

President Lincoln had his eye on what happened at Nashville. So did General Grant. But the responsibility for defending the city, which had been occupied by Union forces for almost three years, lay with Maj. Gen. George H. Thomas, commanding officer of Union forces stationed in Nashville.

A West Point graduate, a deliberate man who plotted his tactics carefully and made no move until he was sure of his ability to finish the job, Thomas was under heavy pressure to hold Nashville at all costs.

The city had fallen into Union hands early in the war, on

February 24, 1862, and in 2 ½ years had been ringed with hilltop fortifications linked by trenches.

Thomas had two lines of defense across the city's southern border. If the outer line—dipping southward as far as what is now Linden Avenue, near Hillsboro Road—should fall, Union troops could withdraw to another defense line, nearer the city.

That line forked off what is now Reservoir Hill (then called Fort Casino), above Eighth Avenue, S., and bent sharply westward and northwestward to encircle what is now downtown Nashville.

Between the outer and inner lines of defense lay a wide band that included what is today much of the Belmont and Hillsboro areas, including part of the Vanderbilt campus and much of Centennial Park and reaching northwest to the Cumberland River.

The main line of defense began at the Cumberland River in South Nashville, near the site of the present General Hospital, and swung up to Fort Negley.

Next hilltop in the ring around Nashville was Reservoir Hill (Fort Casino), and from there the trenches ran up the hill at Fifteenth and Ashwood, where TV station WDCN stood until recently. (Union Gen. Benjamin Harrison, later to become president of the United States, commanded Federal forces in the line between Reservoir Hill and the old television station.)

Before the war, Fort Negley was called St. Cloud Hill, and its grove of oak trees made it a favorite picnic area. Union soldiers cleared out the trees on that and other hills in their line of defense; from those shaved hilltops they could get an unobstructed view in all directions.

From Reservoir Hill, there was a clear view to Fort Negley to the northeast, to the hill where the WDCN studio stood later, and to the tower of the Belmont mansion which stands today as the nucleus of the Belmont College campus. That tower served as signal point for Federal forces.

From there the outer Union line swept southwest toward a hill near Linden and Eighteenth Avenue, S. (Early in the battle General Thomas stood on this hill to survey the action.)

Sweeping further west from there, the Union line rose to the high hill topping Love Circle and ended at the river, near the grounds of Tennessee State University.

Both Union General Thomas, commanding over 70,000 men (55,000 in actual combat), and Confederate Gen. John Bell Hood, commanding 23,000 troops, had planned their battle tactics well in advance.

When it would start was a matter of weather, as far as Thomas was concerned. He had the men, the horses, the guns, the ammunition, the clothing, the food, the medical supplies. He would have attacked the Confederate army approaching from the south two weeks earlier if it had not been for the snow, ice, and bitter cold that made it impossible for men and horses to climb the steep slopes.

For the Confederate army, torn and spent from fearsome losses at the Battle of Franklin on November 30 and from long months of fighting their way northward after the Battle of Atlanta, every day counted in their feeble attempts to build some sort of defenses of their own.

Surveying the formidable defense lines that the Union forces had built across the city's southern border, Hood correctly predicted what Union tactics would be: to unleash a mighty army from the west and hurl it straight across the Hillsboro Pike.

So Hood had his Confederate troops busy building breastworks on top of five hilltops along Hillsboro Pike. They were, for the most part, dug out some four or five feet below the topmost rim of the hill.

Those hilltop entrenchments were called redoubts, and Hood designated them Redoubts No. 1, 2, 3, 4, and 5. They covered a two-mile stretch of Hillsboro Road, including the valley where Green Hills Shopping Center thrives today.

Inside each redoubt were usually four howitzers with as many as forty-eight men to fire them, and another one hundred men to protect the gunners.

The idea behind those fortified hilltops was that Confederate cannons could sweep across the valleys between them and clear out any attacking Union forces.

The redoubt nearest the city, Redoubt No. 1, stood on a hill that rises above what is now Benham Avenue (running off Stokes Lane, between Hillsboro and Belmont).

The last of Hood's series of five redoubts stood on a hill near Harding Place, just west of Hillsboro Road, where row upon row of town houses of Jefferson Square rise along the slopes today.

The population of Nashville (exclusive of the 100,000 military) was 30,000 then, and the city limits were no farther from the river than Twelfth Avenue.

So the entire area of the battle was open farmland, dominated by a few great mansions like Belle Meade and Belmont, and less pretentious homes like Travelers Rest and the Compton homes—all of which can be seen today.

On Hillsboro Pike, there was the Felix Compton home (now the A. M. Burton home, at 5050 Hillsboro Road), across the road from Redoubt No. 5. The Compton home, with its tall square columns across the front, was to have its broad lawns fought over and its staircase nicked by bullets.

Most of the people who lived in Nashville were Confederate sympathizers, and it was apparent from his preparation that Confederate General Hood had reliable sources of information about when the Union forces would strike.

For one thing, the ice and snow that had gripped the city for two weeks began to thaw. Man and horse could begin to move about on steadier footing.

So on Wednesday afternoon, December 14, Union General Thomas assembled his officers in his rooms to tell them that the battle would begin the next morning. He gave detailed orders and maps, and drilled every officer there on his exact part in the next day's attack.

Reveille would be sounded at 4 A.M., and every Union soldier would have breakfast, break camp, pack, and be on the way to his assigned post by 6 A.M. There would be not only a continuous line of soldiers defending the broad Union lines, but also 55,000 other soldiers free for actual combat.

Close behind every Union division that went on the battlefield there would be five wagonloads of ammunition, ten ambulance wagons, and other wagons loaded with tools for trench digging. Still other wagons and supplies would be kept in reserve inside the lines.

Some Union soldiers were equipped with repeater rifles —a telling advantage since they would fire seven times without being reloaded. (The Confederate army, on the other hand, had to rely on muskets that had to have the powder and Minié balls rammed down the muzzle with a ramrod after each firing.)

General Hood knew that the attack would come on the morning of December 15. The night before he had given his orders for that day, and at 2 A.M. on December 15 Hood was up and preparing for battle.

With one leg lost in battle and one wounded arm in a sling, the tall, sad-eyed general had to be tied in his saddle.

Hood, who had made his headquarters at Travelers Rest for the two weeks before the battle, moved to the Judge John M. Lea farm and rode off to Montgomery Hill, on what is now Cedar Lane, between Hillsboro and Belmont, to observe the unfolding battle.

A cold fog lay low over the city and obscured the hilltops

as he rode, and visibility was poor through the valley and over the ridges until midmorning. But Nashvillians, getting the word that this was the day for the showdown, had scattered to distant hills to see the fight.

On Capitol Hill, where Union soldiers had camped for years in tents along the fortified hillside and had stored supplies in the marble corridors, the Yankee troops stood watching the distant smoke from guns that shook the hills.

But General Hood, who had fortified Montgomery Hill as the point closest to the Union line, had already withdrawn all but a token force from the suburban point. It was too close for comfort.

There, on a commanding hill where Cedar Lane rises sharply to a crest between Hillsboro Road and Belmont Boulevard today, wealthy A. B. Montgomery had a handsome home, center of a 208-acre farm fronting on Granny White Pike and reaching beyond Hillsboro Pike.

Montgomery's graceful brick home stood just below the crest of the hill, on the Belmont side, and the approach to the house, reaching all the way from Granny White Pike, was a fifty-foot-wide avenue bordered by cedar trees— hence the modern name Cedar Lane.

Formal gardens near the house and acres of orchards sloping down the hillside made Montgomery Hill a scene of serene charm.

All of that is gone today, but Nashvillians approaching the hilltop from Hillsboro Road can see the only one of the Montgomery buildings still standing—now a mellow red brick apartment building at 1808 Cedar Lane. In Montgomery's day, that red brick building was used either as slaves' quarters or as the home of the overseer of Montgomery's farm.

Montgomery Hill was destined to mark the beginning of defeat for the Confederates at the Battle of Nashville.

Thursday, December 15, 1864

While Hood sat in his saddle near Montgomery Hill that December 15 morning, surveying his thin line of defense up and down Hillsboro Pike, Union General Thomas had his men moving out like clockwork toward their twenty-mile line of defense.

Thomas checked out of his hotel—the St. Cloud, at Fifth and Church—at 4 A.M., mounted his horse, and rode off to Fort Negley (at the crest of the hill where Cumberland Museum and Science Center stands today) to signal the firing of the cannon that announced the beginning of the battle. Those shells fell where the fairgrounds are today.

As the mists began to lift, Union soldiers at both east and west ends of the line made stabs at the Confederate line, trying their strength. Hood had only a sketchy line of men scattered from Hillsboro Pike westward toward Charlotte Pike and White Bridge Road and on to the river.

At 8 A.M., a skirmish broke out on the western end of the line, as Union cavalry rode out from behind their lines and found spirited opposition. They pushed from Charlotte Pike eastward toward Harding Pike, and over the rich farmland that is now the Belle Meade section of the city.

The Belle Meade mansion itself—center of a gigantic plantation—was caught in the crossfire as soldiers on both sides fought across the front lawn and to the rear of the house. Today bullet scars in the columns of the house attest to that fierce encounter.

But that was only a jockeying for position. The real task that the Union army had set itself that day was to knock out each end of the Confederate line and then move in on the center with a devastating blow.

All during the morning—in fact, all day long—Union cannons poured out their thunder, and their artillery kept up a bombardment that crackled across the valleys and hills "like canebrake on fire."

By 10 A.M., the Union plan of battle began to take shape. Like spokes of a wheel, the long lines of Federal troops fanned out from their hub (near Twenty-first and Blair) to their rim (near what is now Harding Place).

Moving cautiously through the morning, Union troops were forming a great wedge, with its apex pointing toward town and its opposite side like the rounded rim of a wheel.

The spokes of the wheel were made up of massive units of Union cavalry, infantry, and artillery, and they were geared to pound the Hillsboro Pike entrenchments with heavy artillery fire before the infantry and cavalry rushed the hills to finish off the task.

Confederate soldiers—about 150 of them huddled behind the flimsy protection at each of the five redoubts along Hillsboro Pike—were also entrenched behind the rock wall that ran along the east side of the pike.

Long before the Confederates could see the great sweep of 40,000 Union soldiers moving across the fields from Harding Pike toward Hillsboro, they heard the crackle of their guns.

And then they saw their blue coats, warm against the penetrating dampness, and the Union flags waving.

Union Gen. Thomas J. Wood, commanding troops at the center of the line, had 13,256 bearing hard on Hillsboro, and he wrote glowingly of the spectacle:

"When the grand army of troops began to move forward in unison, the pageant was magnificently grand and imposing. Far as the eye could reach, the lines and masses of blue, over which the nation's emblem flaunted proudly, moved forward in such perfect order that the heart of the patriot might easily draw from it the happy presage of the coming glorious victory."

First punch at that Confederate line came at Montgomery Hill. It was shortly after noon, and Union soldiers approaching the hilltop breastworks had no way of knowing that the Confederates had already abandoned it, except for a few soldiers posted there as lookout.

So the Union forces pounded the breastworks near the old Montgomery farmhouse for some time, and then a brigade was ordered to storm the hill. Surprised by lack of fire as they rushed up the slope, the Union brigade swept up the battered hillside, climbed over the deserted entrenchments—and Montgomery Hill was theirs.

That was only a prelude to other easy victories that Union soldiers were sure would follow quickly.

Early in the afternoon, the southernmost part of the Union "wheel"—the rim, that is—rolled up out of the valley west of Hillsboro Pike and faced the Confederate-held hill whose fortifications were designated Redoubt No. 5.

Jefferson Square town houses and condominiums cover that hill today. Rising high above Hillsboro Road, on the western side, near the intersection with Harding Place, the hill gives a breathtaking view of the city to the west and north.

Jefferson Square residents can look out from their wide-windowed perches at the top of the hill and see the terrain that the 150 Confederate soldiers manning the fortification saw that December 15, 1864. But only in their imagination can they feel what must have been in Confederate minds as thousands of bluecoated Union soldiers swarmed across the valley toward them.

Confederate soldiers on the crest of the hill kept firing away as fast as their muskets could be reloaded. Union cavalrymen rushing toward them cleared the way with their Spencer repeating rifles.

Both armies fired their artillery for about an hour, and then, as the Union soldiers neared the crest, the Confederates gave it all they had.

Even so, the encounter was brief, and the Union soldiers swarmed over the breastworks, overpowered the Confederates inside, and captured their guns and practically all of the men.

The fall of Redoubt No. 5 left Jefferson Square Hill wide open for attack from the Confederates entrenched on a nearby hill, just above Hobbs Road, on what is now Trimble Road. That position, called Redoubt No. 4 in the Confederate line of defense, would be in the backyard of the home at 3333 Trimble Road today.

From there, the four howitzers on the hill were in good position to fire on the higher Redoubt No. 5 and the Union soldiers who had captured it. And there developed the most desperately contested fight in the whole Hillsboro Pike line of battle.

For a young Confederate officer, Capt. Charles L. Lumsden, in charge of Redoubt No. 4, took quite literally the orders to hold that position "at all hazard."

For three hours, Lumsden and his 100 infantrymen defended the hill that had four Napoleon guns (cannons) pouring out shrapnel. But sweeping over their slight hill came 1,200 enemy infantrymen, plus four regiments of cavalry, and their four cannons and hailstorms of artillery fire pulverized the hill.

Pounded by three batteries of guns 600 yards to the west and almost surrounded by the enemy, Lumsden drove his men to almost superhuman effort.

Not until Union soldiers climbed over the breastworks did Lumsden order his men to "take care of yourselves." Only then did they make a dash for Hillsboro Pike and the cover of the rock wall that ran along its eastern side, in the area that is Green Hills Shopping Center today.

It was later that afternoon that Lumsden found in his beard part of the brains of one of his bravest soldiers, killed in those last moments at Redoubt No. 4.

With Redoubts No. 5 and 4 fallen to Union forces, the fight spilled across Hillsboro Pike to the broad sweep of lawn leading to what was then the Felix Compton home (now the A. M. Burton house). A bullet mark on the balustrade of the stairway in the Burton home today is the only relic of the fighting that fanned out across that hill.

Meantime fresh contingents of Union troops rushed from the west toward Redoubt No. 3, an entrenchment on the hill where Calvary United Methodist Church stands today.

As a Union brigade approached this hill (where part of the Confederate breastworks can be seen today) they were met with heavy fire.

But the encounter was brief. Union forces stormed the hill and soon had it under their command. And then Union Col. Sylvester G. Hill—highest-ranking Union officer to lose his life at the Battle of Nashville—was killed. He had just given the order to charge Redoubt No. 2 when a bullet pierced his brain.

That Redoubt No. 2, on a hill that rises east of Hillsboro Road, between the present Woodmont Boulevard and Graybar Lane, had been abandoned just before Union soldiers charged.

It was after Redoubt No. 2 fell that, at about 4:30 in the winter afternoon, Union forces approached Redoubt No. 1 —the closest to the Federal line.

That hill, now grown over with underbrush high above a quiet residential street called Benham (between Stokes Lane and Woodmont), commanded a view reaching from the Belmont area northeast of it to the Hillsboro area west of it, plus dramatic slopes to the north and south.

Union forces, recognizing Redoubt No. 1 as a key point in the Confederate defense and having no idea that it had already been deserted by Confederate soldiers, bombarded it mercilessly, tearing up the breastworks.

At last the Union forces charged the hill and found it empty. By that time the winter darkness was closing in, and there was little for either army to do but try to find their units on the confused battlefield. Both Union and Confederate brigades were scattered from Hillsboro Pike to Granny White and Franklin pikes, and there was a full night's work before them.

Union General Thomas rode his horse back to downtown Nashville to send telegrams of triumph to headquarters in Washington. He doubted that the badly mauled Confederates would fight again the next day.

Grant sent a telegram to Thomas to congratulate him on the day's smashing victory, but he told him to keep after "the enemy until he is entirely destroyed."

President Lincoln wired Thomas "the nation's thanks."

General Hood, in his tent near the John M. Lea home on what is now Lealand Lane, spent the night in preparation for a day that he knew could be saved only by a miracle.

Hood had ridden to the top of what would soon be known as Shy's Hill (as a result of the next day's battle) in the twilight of December 15 and selected it as the western anchor of the Confederate line for the next day's fight.

He had Confederate soldiers building breastworks at the top of the steep "conical hill" through the night, and he had two of Turner's battery cannons pulled up the thawing, muddy slopes that seemed a mountain to the men climbing it. From that height, Hood thought, they could command the surrounding hills and valleys.

Friday, December 16, 1864

Hood tightened his line to a 2 ½-mile stretch reaching roughly from Shy's Hill (near what is now Harding Place and Shy's Hill Road) on the western end to Peach Orchard Hill on the east (a high, rocky ridge that was part of the

John Overton farm then and is cut through now by Interstate 65-S near its intersection with Harding Place).

That battle line, running slightly south of what is now Battery Lane, included a stone fence that was then a dividing line between the farm of Judge John M. Lea and a neighbor. It is today the border of a bridle path between Granny White Pike and Franklin Road, and runs between quiet suburban lawns.

But the stone wall was a solid fortification for Confederate troops that December 16, as they crouched on its southern side, fighting back against Union forces that rained bullets at them all day.

Hood had some of his men entrenched on a hill south of Shy's Hill, and he counted on them to help protect the latter. The hills nearby, almost encircling Shy's Hill, had bristled with activity through the icy night as horses and men struggled to pull their heavy guns to the hilltops.

But in the darkness the Confederate engineers made a fatal mistake that night on Shy's Hill. They miscalculated the position of the infantry line emplaced at the crest of the hill—failing to realize that a plateau jutting out from the slope near the hilltop cut off any view of Union soldiers who might approach from below.

By the time the Confederates discovered their mistake, at daybreak, it was too late. Union troops, quickly taking a neighboring hill, soon were in a position to fire on the Confederates from three directions.

Marooned on their almost defenseless summit, the small contingent on Shy's Hill took what cover they could, hoping for darkness and escape. By noon, they were surrounded by Union forces on three sides, and, as one of the Southerners wrote later, "the Yankee bullets and shell were coming from all directions, passing one another in the air."

Meantime, at the eastern end of the Confederate line, things were going better.

During the night of December 15, Confederate soldiers

at Peach Orchard Hill had made their entrenchments along the top of the crest secure.

By morning, General Thomas had his Union army formed in a continuous line, facing the Confederate line and extending around its two ends.

On the morning of December 16, the Union artillery hailed the day with heavy fire up and down the line, and they never let up all day.

During the morning, Union troops made several feeler attacks on Peach Orchard Hill, but Confederate Gen. Stephen D. Lee, in charge of the men defending that area, beat them back.

By noon, a cold rain began falling, but that did not dampen the spirits of the Union soldiers—including many blacks in the brigades commanded by Gen. J. B. Steedman.

Beaten back at first, the greatly augmented forces fighting under Steedman made another charge up Peach Orchard Hill about 3 o'clock that afternoon—sure of victory this time.

"Full of enthusiasm . . . in splendid array," a Union general reported later, their troops began the climb up the ridge.

But they were "welcomed with a most terrific fire of grape and canister and musketry," from the higher slopes, and they soon encountered even heavier pounding from the Confederate breastworks on top of the ridge.

From that high advantage, a Union general reported later, the Confederates "rose and poured in a fire before which no troops could live."

One officer there said he had "seen most of the battlefields of the West, but never saw dead men thicker" than at Peach Orchard Hill.

Confederate General Lee, commanding the victorious troops, reported simply that the enemy "were driven back in great disorder," and their loss was "very severe."

It was so severe that Peach Orchard Hill was blue with

the bodies of the dead and wounded, and, according to some observers, it would have been possible to walk down the hill by stepping from one bluecoated body to the next.

But that was the only Confederate victory of the day.

At the opposite end of the line, on Shy's Hill, the Confederate soldiers marooned on the hilltop had a range of fire not more than five to twenty yards. They would not be able to shoot at the enemy until he had mounted the hill and was almost upon them.

Confederate soldiers there called it the longest day of their lives. Trees crashed in the shelling around them, and the bullets fell so thick that, according to one of the survivors, "a snowbird could not have lived on that hill."

"If a man raised his head over the slight works, he was very apt to lose it," James L. Cooper, then a twenty-year-old Confederate soldier, recalled years later.

They knew the enemy was creeping up the hill, toward them. They could almost feel their presence.

"A boy could shoot a marble to where they knew a large force was being concentrated to make a dash at them," Cooper wrote.

"Every old ragged Reb, as he lay there during that long day and watched the enemy in full view working around to our left and rear, knew that we would 'light out' as soon as dark."

Gen. Benton Smith, commanding the hilltop troops, "would occasionally send some reckless gallant soul (there were lots of them there covered by those old dirty rags) to creep to the edge of the hill and report the progress of the affair," Cooper recalled.

"They would bring back such cheerful items as 'Can't see down that hollow for the Yankees.' Or, 'They'll give us hell directly.'

"To an unprejudiced mind, they had been giving us that all afternoon."

The rain that had begun about noon fell in sheets

throughout much of the afternoon, and the wet men searched the sky for early darkness and a chance for escape.

Shortly after 4 P.M., "what had been feared occurred."

Out of the deep ravine lying out of the range of Confederate sight or fire, at a point which today lies below the intersection of Harding Place and Shy's Hill Road, a great wave of thousands of Union soldiers began their overwhelming rush up Shy's Hill.

Union Gen. James H. Wilson said his "dismounted troopers had closed in upon the enemy's entrenchments and entered them from the rear before the infantry reached them in front.

"It was now raining heavily, mist was gathering, and dark was closing down like a pall over both victor and vanquished."

Another Union general, A. J. Smith, told of the stealthy climb of his men up the north side of the hill as the Confederates trapped there by fire from three sides fought back "with a fierce storm of shell, canister, and musketry, sadly decimating the ranks of many [Union] regiments, but nothing could stop the progress of that line. . . .

"Sweeping forward, the right of the line up the hill and the left through mud and over the walls, they gained the enemy's works . . . The enemy were whipped, broken and demoralized. Prisoners were taken by the regiment and artillery by batteries."

But Confederates on the hill did not give up without a mighty fight.

Confederate Gen. William B. Bate told of the way his men were boxed in by Union forces arranged like three sides of a square, with Union firing coming in on them from the two parallel sides. He placed his bravest men in position to resist the attack.

"They stood firm and received the fire from three directions with coolness and courage," General Bate wrote.

"Not, however, until the gallant and obstinate Col. William M. Shy and nearly half of his brave men had fallen," along with the largest part of survivors of the other companies, did Union forces capture the hill.

Shy's fighting had fired his men to tremendous effort that December dusk as almost half of the men died in a rain that was soon to turn to sleet.

But at last Shy caught a bullet between the eyes, and his men lost all hope. About half were already dead, and the courage they had shown led even the Union men to refer to it as Shy's Hill from that day on. (Shy's Hill, Hood's Hill Road, General Bate Drive, Battery Lane, and Battlefield Drive are only a fraction of the names that bear testimony to the fighting there.)

Colonel Shy's body was brought to what is now the A. M. Burton home, at 5050 Hillsboro Road, until his family in Franklin could claim it.

Shy's Hill was strewn with the bodies of young men who lost their lives that December 16. Out of one command of one hundred men, sixty-five survived. Others were "nearly annihilated."

Many others were captured. One of them, Gen. Thomas Benton Smith, fought doggedly to hold Shy's Hill, but finally realized it was impossible and commanded his men to surrender. He was disarmed, placed under guard, and escorted about 700 yards to the rear of the Union line.

There, as the twenty-five-year-old General Smith stood, waiting for further orders, a Union officer struck him across the face with a saber, beat him to the ground, and laid his skull open with deep gashes.

Surprisingly, young General Smith recovered from the severe wounds and was held prisoner until the end of the war. But his mind never recovered, and he spent much of his long life as a mental patient at Central State Hospital. Sometimes he was well enough to attend Confederate reunions, and at the gathering of his old regiment, the Twentieth Tennessee, it is said he could call the roll from memory as long as he lived.

He was eighty-four years old when he died in 1923, and he was buried in the shadow of an imposing Confederate monument in Confederate Circle on a hilltop at Mt. Olivet Cemetery. In 1955, a street that winds around Shy's Hill was named in his honor—Benton Smith Road.

But at that bloody defeat in the twilight at Shy's Hill, nobody was thinking of memorials. They were fighting for their lives, and, as James Cooper said, "our men and the enemy were so mixed they could not be told apart."

One by one, the beaten Confederates turned and fled down the muddy slopes, heading across the cornfields for a low pass, Cheatham's Gap, between the Overton hills, in hopes of escape out Granny White Pike or Franklin Pike toward the south.

"All of the enemy that did escape were pursued over the tops of Brentwood and Harpeth Hills," Union General Thomas reported later.

One Confederate general, H. R. Jackson, tried to find his way to the place where he had left his horse, but the mud chewed by wagons and horses was a foot deep and caked so thick on his boots that he stopped to knock it off.

Suddenly General Jackson, with one boot off, was surrounded by the enemy, with guns pointed at him. When he surrendered, the Yankee corporal nearest tossed his hat in the air and yelled triumphantly, "Captured a general, by God! I will take you to Nashville myself."

When Shy's Hill collapsed, the whole line joined the stampede southward. And General Hood, seated on his horse not far from the center of the line along what is now Lealand Lane, was shocked at the suddenness of the collapse.

"I beheld for the first and only time a Confederate army

abandon the field in confusion," Hood wrote of that stunned moment.

Along the routes of escape, there were still moments of heroism—of men like Gen. Stephen D. Lee who tried to stop the panicked onrush of defeated Confederates.

"Rally, men! For God's sake, rally," General Lee called at one point, as he stirred drummer boys to roll the drums and flagbearers to show the colors through the icy rain. "This is the place for brave men to die."

But the rushing hundreds of Confederates, pursued by thousands of Union soldiers, knew defeat when they saw it. General Lee's attempt at a rally at Hollow Tree Gap (seven miles north of Franklin) at 10 P.M. failed.

On Granny White Pike, there was fierce hand-to-hand fighting in the darkness, and two mounted colonels on opposite sides of a rock wall bordering the road fought with saber and gun.

At midnight, the two armies stopped where they were, and one injured soldier, seeking out General Hood to ask for a leave, found the gaunt-faced man distraught in his tent, between Nashville and Franklin.

"He was much agitated and affected, pulling his hair with one hand (he had but one) and crying like his heart would break," the young soldier wrote of the beaten Hood that night.

For ten days more the Yankee pursuit of the Rebels was to take the latter through nightmares of rain, ice, sleet, and snow; of deep ruts cut through muddy roads; of men freezing and bleeding and dying.

Union General Thomas reported that the two days' fighting at Nashville had cost him 387 dead, 2,562 wounded, and 112 missing. He said he had captured 4,462 Confederates.

Federal troops listed on duty for that battle numbered 70,272, of whom 55,000 took part in the battle.

There were 23,000 Confederates in the Battle of Nashville. Nobody knows exactly how many were killed.

Soldiers who passed along the frozen road strewn with lifeless, maimed bodies the next day said they would never be able to erase the scene of horror from their minds.

Episcopal Bishop Charles T. Quintard (later a founder of the University of the South at Sewanee) was a young chaplain and physician in the Confederate army. After the Battle of Nashville, sickened by the suffering around him, he turned from the burial of fellow soldiers to write in his diary of that December horror:

> *Alas for our poor bleeding land,*
> *Alas for the friends I mourn,*
> *Darkest of all Decembers*
> *Ever my life has known.*

Nashville's Biggest Party

It was almost midnight on a balmy Saturday, October 30, 1897, and the last fireworks arching the sky over the Parthenon had sputtered out.

The crowds on the brilliantly lighted Centennial grounds were suddenly silent too.

For that night, more than eighty years ago, was the final night of Tennessee's gigantic, six-month-long celebration of her 100th birthday.

And the crowds, melancholy at the closing of the joyous spectacle, could not bear the thought of giving up the Parthenon, heart and symbol of the Centennial celebration.

There was talk of keeping the Parthenon, even when the other thirty-five buildings on the Centennial grounds were torn down. Then perhaps the grounds could be preserved as a public park.

"The question is: Are these grounds to be a monument to the Exposition?" said Tully Brown, civic leader and orator on that final program. "Are we going to make this a public park?"

"Yes! Yes!" the cheering thousands answered.

"Who will be the man to strike the first blow to the Parthenon?" he persisted.

"No! Never!" the crowd shouted back.

So Nashville never did tear down its proud Parthenon— except to replace the aging original wood-and-plaster building with the present concrete duplicate. And today tourists and newcomers to Nashville who are puzzled by the stately hunk of concrete can hardly imagine what love, sweat, and tears were built into those walls.

The idea for the building came from Maj. Eugene Castner Lewis, a peppery little businessman-engineer whose genius has left a strong imprint on Nashville—including the entire city park system.

But Major Lewis (who won his title when he was a hot-tempered Tennessee schoolboy defying Yankee soldiers during the Civil War) did not get his chance at planning buildings and grounds for the Centennial celebration until the difficult financial groundwork had been laid.

As early as August 10, 1892, a young Nashville lawyer, Douglas Anderson, was writing letters to newspapers throughout the state, suggesting that Tennessee should be the first in the Union to hold a great exposition to celebrate her 100th birthday.

Tennessee was poor. She was suffering from a painful depression. And the Centennial would "redound to the pecuniary benefit of the State, and keep alive State Pride."

The pecuniary benefit was the tantalizing bait. Jobs were scarce, salaries low, investment money tight. Businessmen and city and state officials doubted that it was possible to raise enough money to stage such a celebration.

Not until the railroads of Nashville took up the challenge was there any chance of undertaking it.

J. B. Killebrew, who had been state commissioner of agriculture, went before the legislature to plead for support of the statewide celebration. He was convinced that the exhibits would spur Tennesseans to venture into industry—to produce some of their own shoes, hats, plows, and wagons, for instance.

Killebrew argued that farmers would have a ready market close to Tennessee factories. They could save on freight, and become shippers rather than consumers.

Men of means from other parts of the country would see the promise in Tennessee's many resources if there were an exposition in Nashville, Killebrew said. They would invest in the new industry.

But the legislature sat on its purse, and so did Nashville's city council, for three years. Finally, in July, 1895—less than a year from the date of the proposed celebration—labor unions, civic organizations, and Nashville businesses subscribed $165,000 toward the project. As it turned out, it took $1,101, 246.40 to get the job done. Private subscriptions made it all possible.

The railroads with lines into Nashville, particularly the Nashville, Chattanooga & St. Louis Railway, became solid backers. Convinced that the celebration would bring both immediate and long-term profits (through passengers and increased freight shipment), they cut their rates drastically and arranged excursions from all parts of the United States. Altogether the railroads contributed $167,000 to the Centennial.

So it was no coincidence that, when the Centennial Exposition was finally organized on July 23, 1895, the president of the N. C. & St. L. Railway, John W. Thomas, was also elected president of the Centennial.

Thomas, then an impressive-looking man of sixty-five years, was a Nashville native, much revered from Civil War days when, as a young ticket agent at Murfreesboro, he had helped move Confederate soldiers and supplies.

In the days when no public event in Nashville was complete without a parade including Confederate veterans, Thomas went out of his way to honor them. His name, for that reason and countless others, won instant loyalty to any project he headed.

But Thomas said he would not undertake the job as president of the Centennial unless Major Lewis became director general. Lewis accepted that job, and so undertook the enormous task of planning all buildings, grounds, exhibits, police and fire protection, and hospital facilities.

Lewis, a bright-eyed, slight man who walked fast, talked fast, was "straight as an arrow and looked like a little dancing master," made tough men tremble with his brusque ways and tart tongue.

"He was a genius—a peculiar man, but a genius," Frederick Whittemore, one of his former business associates, said. "He was brilliant, eccentric, positive."

At the time of the Centennial, he was chief engineer (in charge of planning all railroad lines) and was later president of the railroad. He bought *The Nashville American* to promote the Centennial.

At the same time he was engaged in Centennial plans, Lewis was working on designs for the present Union Station (completed in 1900), and the Church Street and Broadway viaducts.

He plunged into plans for the Centennial full force—searching for a theme that would excite Tennesseans. He had no patience with suggestions that the celebration take the coonskin and log-cabin theme. He wanted an exposition that would point to the future, and would do it in light, clean-lined buildings, free of the gingerbread architecture that he abhorred.

Lewis read the classics avidly, and pored over his drawing board at such unpredictable moments that he had one set up in his bedroom for middle-of-the-night ideas. To overcome his insomnia, he had a bed swung from the ceiling on chains, and—in spite of the effort to relax—he collapsed twice before the Centennial was finished.

But six weeks from the time he was appointed director general, Lewis had the plans worked out, ready to present to the meeting of the executive committee on September 12, 1895.

What more appropriate symbol for the "Athens of the

South," he asked, than a replica of the Parthenon, crowning architectural jewel of Greece's classical era?

After all, as early as 1825, soon after Philip Lindsley came to Nashville as president of Davidson College, he referred to the college-heavy town as the "Athens of the South." Felix Grundy, distinguished lawyer and congressman, used the same term at about the same time.

When Lewis proposed the Parthenon as central building of the Centennial, with all the other buildings clustered about it and a lake to reflect it, the executive board was stunned by his idea.

"So lucid, comprehensive, and admirable was this well considered scheme that the executive committee at once adopted his plans by a unanimous vote . . . as an expression of confidence in the powers of the creative genius who had undertaken the stupendous work," Herman Justi wrote later in his *Official History of the Tennessee Centennial Exposition.*

Lewis turned to the British Museum for exact floor plans for the Parthenon (dedicated to the goddess Athene in 438 B.C. and reduced to ruins in an explosion of gunpowder stored there in 1687).

Lewis, a thrifty man pinching hard-won Centennial pennies, paid $500 for two rare volumes filled with detailed drawings of the Parthenon in Athens. From them came precise studies of optical illusion in the construction of the Parthenon. From them came the realization that no two columns in the building were exactly the same, and that all of them bulged in the middle to create the illusion of straight lines.

The executive committee had leased West Side Park, a 135-acre race-track area just west of Vanderbilt University campus, as the site for the Exposition. Its broad acres were shaded by giant trees, and the site would be easily accessible by streetcar and train—the latter running from the Church Street depot near Ninth Avenue to the north side of the park.

A white-columned railway station was built at the park entrance, and trains could shuttle passengers between downtown Nashville and the Centennial grounds in five minutes.

Lewis considered placing the Parthenon on the hill northwest of the chosen site, but abandoned that location because he thought the hill—though reminiscent of the Greek setting—would be difficult for some visitors to climb.

He scooped out land for the lake and used that soil to build up a mound to gain some elevation for the Parthenon. On October 8, 1895, the cornerstone for the Parthenon was laid, and Lewis saw to it that the ceremony marking the beginning of that first building was lavishly publicized.

A master promoter, he had organized a parade of military units and civic leaders from the Public Square to the Parthenon site. There were speeches by Gov. Peter Turney and other distinguished officials.

Mrs. J. W. Thomas, wife of the Centennial president, tapped the cornerstone three times with a "beautiful gavel of gilded steel, with a blue ribbon tied about the handle," and pronounced the dedicatory words:

"I dedicate the building, of which this is the cornerstone, to the honor and memory of those heroic men and women who braved the perils of frontier life and in 1796 founded the State of Tennessee."

Already the Centennial board had realized they could not get all the buildings completed, the grounds landscaped, and the exhibitions in place in time to open the Exposition in June, 1896—the actual 100th birthday of Tennessee.

So they voted to have the Exposition open one year later. And for eighteen months work on the Parthenon and other tremendous buildings proceeded.

It was to be a "White City," with all of the buildings made of wood, covered with plaster, and painted white. There were exhibition buildings covering a wide variety of interests, and each was of a different architectural style.

Memphis, building her own exhibition hall near the Parthenon, designed it in the shape of a pyramid. Texas, for its exhibits, made a replica of the Alamo. Mexico, for her exhibits of brilliantly woven fabrics and pottery of wide variety, constructed an Aztec-styled building with cactus plants nearby.

There were huge buildings like the Commerce Building, the Woman's Building, the Agriculture Building, and the Negro Building that had to have walkways and landscaping planned to make them accessible from streets and walks.

There were tiny buildings like the nursery (where parents could leave their children for fifty cents a day) and the hospital (where doctors and nurses on duty around the clock took care of an average of thirty-eight patients daily).

Lewis faced a major job in designing and building the lakes, dams, bridges, grottoes, fountains, roads, and walks to create exotic scenes from many lands. There were real gondolas on the lake and gondoliers imported from Venice to propel visitors around it. There were reproductions of Venetian bridges, and camels from Cairo to give visitors a ride in the Egyptian area.

But the marvel of it all, it turned out, was the electric lighting. On opening night, when every building was outlined in rows of lights and the whole scene reflected in the mirroring Lake Watauga, the crowds gasped in admiration. The magic, the excitement of the White City by night, never wore off.

To furnish all of that electric power—plus the power for lighting exhibits inside every building—the Centennial had its own power plant, and was proud of the fact that it never broke down during the whole six-month celebration.

In the same Machinery Building—a powerful attraction in itself—were not only the power generators, but also the electric pumps used to pump water from the city mains far away. The lakes on the grounds were filled from springs.

Lewis had the lakes and statuary spotlighted for drama and romance at night, and so arranged between the forest trees and shrubs that there was always a shady spot to avoid the midday sun.

There were park benches under the trees, and inviting stretches of grass for spreading picnics. There were restaurants to appeal to every taste: those that served German food, French food, Italian food, Chinese food, and old southern standbys.

When the question arose about serving beer at German restaurants, and wine at French and Italian restaurants, dry Nashville was up in arms for a while. The Centennial board solved that problem by having a special bill put through the legislature to create a new city—"Centennial City"—for the duration of the celebration.

There, in what was for a few months the most sophisticated city in the state, the restaurants served beer and wine. Centennial City also had its own police force—never less than 88 on duty in one day, and sometimes as many as 135. A fire department was also set up on the grounds and put out several small restaurant blazes.

And Centennial City had its own newspaper, *The Centennial News,* published weekly for almost a year. Major Lewis himself was in charge of all promotion for the Centennial for over a year. A showman with keenest instinct for the proper handling of publicity, he not only scheduled a constant succession of newsworthy events but also saw to it that newspapers in this country and abroad were kept well informed on every detail.

Lewis left nothing undone to please the press. He knew their enthusiasm would bring trainloads of visitors in from

all over the country, and he attracted to Nashville corre-
spondents from *The London Times, The New York Times, The
Chicago Times-Herald,* and newspapers in Boston, Baltimore,
Washington, Seattle, New Orleans, and half a dozen papers
in Europe.

Lewis saw to it that the Press Building on the Centennial
grounds had its own telegraph office, telephones, and type-
writers for visiting newsmen. The ninety-four "incandes-
cent lights" in the building made it the best lighted on the
grounds.

Housed in a "comfortable little Queen Anne cottage,"
near the center of the grounds, the Press Building had "all
the facilities, including a porch from which reporters had
a good view of all parades."

Herman Justi, who was in charge of the fair's promotion
department, had six assistants, and they not only published
the weekly paper but also flooded the nation's press associations and newspapers with news releases, folders, and
pamphlets that kept the world informed of the progress of
the Centennial celebration.

And even if the Centennial had to be postponed to 1897,
there was a two-day celebration of Tennessee's actual
100th birthday, June 1, 1896.

Lewis saw that day as a magnificent prelude to the real
celebration, and he had so many special trains running into
Nashville from all over the state, at bargain rates, that every
hotel, boardinghouse, and private home was packed to capacity.

Downtown streets were draped in bunting, and state and
national flags were flying all along the city's streets, both
residential and business.

On that Monday morning, June 1, 1896, at sunrise, a
sixteen-gun salute from Capitol Hill signified that Tennessee was the sixteenth state to enter the Union (the last state
admitted while George Washington was president).

"By 6 A.M., the streets were packed and jammed with visitors," *The Nashville American* reported. "But the rain came in torrents for hours, and the people had to seek shelter."

The big parade was scheduled for 9 A.M., but it had to be postponed from hour to hour. All morning long, the question was: Will the parade go on? The Centennial board kept meeting again and again as the rain fell. Crowds in hotel lobbies and stores sent messengers to the newspaper-office billboard, in front of the building, to see the latest bulletins posted there.

At length the announcement came: The parade would begin at noon, no matter what the weather. Soon the news was all over town. (Nashville's population at that time was under 100,000, and Eighth Avenue—then Spruce Street— was in the heart of the fashionable residential area.)

"Blasts from the buglers' trumpets announced the soldiers were moving," *The American* reported. "The rain ceased. The clouds scattered. Blasts from the bugles soon reached the whole city. . . . The whole population sprang to life."

The papers estimated that 125,000 people watched the parade of 10,000 people march by, from the Public Square to the Centennial grounds.

Through the muddy streets came the mounted officers, the cavalry units, the infantry, the Marine band with its marvelous marching music, the Confederate Veterans, Gov. Bob Taylor, distinguished guests, and officials of the Centennial by the carriageload.

Newspapermen from Washington, New York, Philadelphia, Baltimore, Boston, Seattle, Chicago, Cleveland, Buffalo, Pittsburgh, and New Orleans joined Tennessee newsmen in covering the event. *Harpers* magazine sent artists to sketch the opening events, and writers to cover it.

For two days there were concerts and speeches, fireworks

and guns fired—not only 100 times for the 100 years of Tennessee history, but also for each of the states then in the Union.

Only two of the Centennial buildings were completed then—the high-domed Auditorium, where the important speeches and ceremonies took place; and the elegant Woman's Building, where a grand stairway and handsome reception rooms set the stage for entertaining celebrities.

The eleven months after that June 1, 1896, celebration were packed with work to meet the deadline for formal opening of the Centennial. Under the direction of Robert C. Creighton, contractor-engineer in charge of constructing all buildings and all work on the grounds, the 135 acres were transformed into a land of magic. A total of nine large and thirty-five small buildings was packed full of exotic exhibits, and there were great areas set aside for fun and frolic.

To herald the opening day, May 1, 1897, *The Chicago Times-Herald* published a special edition of the paper and sent it by special train, the *Dixie Hummer,* delivering the thousands of copies in record time: eight hours and forty-four minutes from Chicago to Nashville.

High point of that May 1 celebration was the moment that President McKinley, in the White House, stepped across the hall from his office to press the button that fired the opening gun in Nashville.

It was 12:13 P.M., Nashville time, and the thousands who had crowded through the four white-columned gateways to tour the grounds had heard three hours of high-powered oratory from Governor Taylor and the Centennial officials. As the moment neared for the president to touch the button, the crowd grew quiet.

Shattering the silence, a cannon on the Centennial grounds fired, and at the same moment the generating plants were turned on to produce electricity for the six-month Exposition.

"People wild," was the message the telegraph keys in Nashville sent back to McKinley. "The gun went off all right. Bands playing and whistles going. Everybody shakes hands."

The crowd thought of Governor Taylor's speech. He had predicted that the century to come would pack more scientific achievement into its years than man had achieved in the 1,000 years before.

"If our fathers, who died a hundred years ago, could see the miracles that have been wrought, if they could see their children talking across oceans and sweeping across continents in palace cars swifter than the swiftest wings," Governor Taylor said, "I doubt not they would shout for joy and sing with us, 'Praise God from whom all blessings flow.' "

The railroads of the country had a "palace car" on exhibit, and various organizations were permitted to have luncheons and dinners served there.

In the Transportation Building, there were exhibits of the latest in Pullman cars and diners. There were enormous buildings housing international exhibits, exhibits of commerce and manufactures, machinery, history, geology, forestry and forest products, hygiene and medicine, education, livestock, the military, children and Negroes. The building dedicated to the progress of Negroes in Tennessee was of special interest. It was a tribute to the Negro's contribution to Tennessee, and its purpose was "to show the progress of the Negro race in America from the old plantation days to the present."

Every day was devoted to a different city or state, and delegations from that city and state got royal treatment. Conventions were scheduled throughout the six-month Centennial celebration, and they brought everybody from Susan B. Anthony to Booker T. Washington to Nashville.

Special trains ran from Chicago, St. Louis, New Orleans,

and Cincinnati to the fair. The Maxwell House hotel, Nashville's finest, advertised rooms "from $1 up," and a full-course dinner with all the trimmings for $1.

The Tulane Hotel, at Eighth and Church, was the largest in the state, with a "capacity of 750 guests" and rates of "$1 and up."

For those who wanted a bird's-eye view of the Centennial, there was a "giant see-saw" with enclosed cabs at each end, which lifted passengers 200 feet into the air.

And if that height were not terrifying enough, visitors could "Shoot the Chutes"—traveling down an inclined slope in a small seat and landing at the surface of the lake.

"You travel hundreds of feet in five seconds," the ad read. "You feel like you had fallen out of a 40-story window."

For the young men who wanted to see a bit of the naughty world, there were the walled "Streets of Cairo," where dark-eyed belly dancers went through their gyrations in filmy skirts.

There was such an endless display of everything beautiful and exciting for Tennessee's future that people bought season tickets and came back day after day to see more sights.

Young people met there, courted there, decided to marry there. Every afternoon and every night there was a concert by one of America's great bands, and every night there was a display of fireworks that filled the skies with fantastic designs.

Victor Herbert and his famous 22nd Regiment Band, of New York, played every day and night from August 2 to September 7, and their rousing marches—some of them Herbert's own compositions—set a new high for Nashville.

In the daytime, at 4 P.M., the band played inside the auditorium, and at 8 P.M. they played in the open air, in the band Pavilion. And the Bellstedt-Ballenberg Band—a great favorite of the day—played for weeks after the opening of the Centennial.

When President and Mrs. McKinley came to the Centennial, they brought with them a trainload of Ohioans, including their own Cincinnati Marine Band, 100 Cincinnati policemen, the governor of Ohio, the mayor of Cincinnati, and scores of other officials.

That was on June 12, the day set to honor Ohio. The presidential party arrived the day before, stayed at the Maxwell House, and (except for President and Mrs. McKinley) assembled in the lobby at 9 A.M. on June 12.

From there they marched as a body up the Church Street hill to the depot at Ninth and Church. There they boarded a train to the Centennial grounds, were guests of honor at a reception, and proceeded to the Cincinnati Building for the dedication.

Meanwhile, at 10 A.M., President and Mrs. McKinley, escorted by Tennessee's Governor Taylor and the chief officials of the Centennial, left the Maxwell House for a drive through the Vanderbilt campus on their way to the Centennial.

After dedication ceremonies at the Cincinnati Building, President McKinley made a tour of all the chief exhibition buildings and was honored at two receptions.

At the same time, his wife, a frail woman who suffered a seizure before the day was over, was caught up in a series of receptions, luncheon, etc., elaborately planned by the city's leading ladies, in the Woman's Building.

The luncheon for Mrs. McKinley, called the "crowning social event of the Centennial season," was held in the Assembly Hall of the Woman's Building, "in a bewildering profusion of floral decorations."

That included asparagus vines wrapped around the pillars of the room, and "white roses, sweet peas and carnations in crystal vases." The president's wife sat at a crescent-shaped table, with heavy-scented magnolia blossoms and ferns inside the curve of the table, and her chair "wreathed in asparagus vines and tied in the national colors.

"Myriads of tiny electric lights shone like stars from the ceiling," Justi wrote, and white candles in silver candelabra peeped out of the labyrinth of flowers.

Mrs. Van Leer Kirkman, a queenly woman who headed the Woman's Department of the Centennial celebration, presided over the luncheon. Woman's Department officers, wives of Centennial officers and government officials, along with the state's social leaders, sat at the many smaller tables packed into the room.

And then at 6 P.M. the entire presidential party said goodbye to the Centennial, took the train to the Church Street depot, and, after a rest at the Maxwell House, took another train back to Cincinnati that night.

One of the purposes of the Woman's Department of the Centennial was to "enlarge the sphere of woman's activity and influence," and the committee in charge stirred up enough civic consciousness among women to make themselves heard in legislative halls in the years following.

They also accomplished so much, working as a unit for those six months, that the women decided to continue their civic work in a club they founded, the Centennial Club. (That club, long a leader in cultural and social life in Nashville, has a handsome clubhouse now on Abbott Martin Road.)

But the Centennial ladies put on a performance so dripping with rosebuds and lace one day that fall—September 30—that it sounded like something out of knighthood's fantasy. It was Kate Kirkman Day, a day set aside to honor the women of the Centennial and their chairman.

To outdo all other processions of the parade-heavy Centennial, the ladies staged a parade of flowers which, it turned out, was a triumph of floral fantasy.

Hundreds of children in pony carts, ladies in victorias and other traps, and young ladies on bicycles had their vehicles so lined in blossoms and decked in blossoms— from the spokes of the wheels to the bridles of the horses —that the judges had difficulty deciding on prizewinners.

The children were all in white, and the ladies wore puffy-sleeved white or pastel gowns, with ribbons of satin and billowy skirts of tucks and lace.

For weeks before, the "floral parade was the sole topic of society," and the Italian who instructed the ladies in the floral designs assured them they were the same as those used in flower fetes in southern Italy.

"The glories of other days may be forgotten," Justi wrote, "but the warm sunshine and the blue skies, the beauteous panorama that moved through the Centennial Park that afternoon will never cease to move across the canvass of the mind."

Lewis, a stickler for starting every event precisely at the appointed moment, thought the ladies did fairly well in getting their flower-decked carriages ready to enter the parade ground only three minutes late.

At that moment, bugles sounded, "music burst forth," and the ladies in their flower-lined carriages, lined up behind one of the Centennial buildings, drove majestically into parade line.

They proceeded in front of the Parthenon, around Lake Watauga, and on to the judges' box in front of the Woman's Building.

Mrs. Kirkman, "queen of the fete," wore rose-colored moire silk as she rode in a victoria covered with violets.

Mrs. Felix Ewing, who won first prize in the ladies' division, drove a victoria decorated to look like a green basket filled with pink chrysanthemums.

Little Margaret Warner, whose "pony cart was a bed of yellow roses," won first prize in the children's class.

That night, at a grand reception at the Woman's Building, 1,200 invited guests showed up to honor Mrs. Kirkman, who was regal in white satin, "with side trimmings of lace on the skirt, and a corsage embroidered with ostrich feathers outlined with dazzling gems."

On the day set aside to honor Thomas, president of the Centennial, the largest crowd of the Exposition showed up: 98,570 visitors. On the day honoring Major Lewis, a march written in his honor, the "Director-General's March," by Bellstedt, was played for the first time. The fireworks displayed that night were, appropriately, the most elaborate of the whole Exposition.

Over the celebrations flew a gigantic American flag, atop a 250-foot-high pole, and an 18-foot statue of Mercury surveyed the scene from the top of the Commerce Building (the same statue later topped the tower at Union Station).

A tremendous statue of Minerva, goddess of wisdom, stood on the grounds near the west end of the Parthenon, and a statue of Commodore Vanderbilt (since then on the Vanderbilt campus) stood near the east end of the Parthenon.

In October, the last month of the Centennial, there was a great rash of national conventions on the Centennial grounds. Trainloads of visitors came from as far away as Canada and New York, and the New Yorkers later published a booklet recording every day of their week-long trip.

They left New York on Friday, October 8, had stops for sight-seeing along the way, plus royal entertainment while they were in Nashville, and were back in New York the next Friday.

Their special train was a luxury train, with nine Pullman cars, two dining cars, and a smoking car with a men's barbershop and full bath at one end. Staterooms and bedrooms on the train were as comfortable as any modern hotel, the travelers said. And most of them lived on the train, parked right beside the Centennial grounds, during their visit.

The top officials of New York and Brooklyn were aboard, to attend New York State Day and Brooklyn Day ceremonies. They brought along a unit of the Brooklyn National Guards to march in their official parade, and had ten well-known New York editors and reporters to report every detail of the Centennial celebration.

The *Brooklyn Eagle,* in fact, published a special small edition on board the train every day of the trip.

As they sped along, sometimes at fifty miles an hour, they dined luxuriously, partied, devised hilarious games and contests. For prizes at a euchre party, they presented such treasures as "a silk hat brush with solid silver handle" (for men), and "an ivory glove stretcher, mounted with sterling silver" (for women).

Menus, they said, were excellent at every meal on the train and "waiters, cooks, porters, stewards, messengers were polite, courteous, thoroughly alive to the wants of the travelers."

When they woke up just outside the Centennial grounds on Monday morning, they found not only the usual rounds of receptions and parades and speech making, but numerous private parties given in their honor.

One of them was at Colemere, the "charming country seat of Col. and Mrs. Edmund W. Cole," on Murfreesboro Road.

The New Yorkers, riding in a procession of 100 horse-drawn carriages, left the Centennial grounds at 2:30 P.M. that bright October day and were enchanted by the six miles of winding road through a "beautiful, wooded, hilly section" to the house that stood where a private club of the same name stands today near Nashville's airport.

Approaching the house by "a private drive, leading through a magnificent park of rare old trees," the New Yorkers were greeted by the music of a band "stationed on the lawn."

In the reception line at Colemere were Mrs. Cole and her mother, Mrs. Russell, plus many dignitaries and visiting lady writers convening at the Centennial.

The next day, the New Yorkers accepted the invitation of Gen. W. H. Harding to visit his famed horse farm, Belle Meade. They took the train out to Belle Meade, toured the 4,500-acre estate to see 200 wild deer rounded up and to visit the stable housing Iroquois, the $250,000 animal considered "the most valuable horse in the world."

When the "favored few" were invited in to sip "genuine Southern mint julep" with Harding, they felt that they were seeing southern life at its storybook best. And that night, after a final tour of the Centennial, they boarded their train again to pull out of Nashville at midnight for a gala series of parties on the trip back home.

Two weeks later the Centennial was over, and a total of 1,669,579 paid visitors had attended. Moreover—in spite of a yellow fever scare that cut down attendance in midsummer—the Centennial had made money. The Tennessee Centennial was, in fact, the only known exposition in the U.S. ever to have come out with a profit.

When the figures were in, receipts were $1,101,285.84— exactly $39.40 more than the Centennial had spent. Additional assets of about $12,000 came from sale of salvaged material when the buildings were razed.

But the results of the Centennial were incalculable. Nashville did keep the Centennial grounds and turn them into Centennial Park—site of generations of duck feeding, courting, strolling, enjoying the lake and flowers. For years it was the city's largest park—hub and inspiration for the entire park system.

The Parthenon did remain focal point in that park, though the original building became so decrepit in the 1920s that it was replaced, on the same spot, by the present concrete replica, completed in 1931.

And new industries, new social and cultural activities grew out of the exposition. New families settled in Nashville. The railroads, which had undertaken the major burden of making the Centennial a success, reaped a rich harvest—never dreaming that automobiles would soon make them almost as obsolete as the stagecoach.

The bond between the men who had worked together to see the Centennial through grew stronger with the years. Two years after the Centennial closed, all of the men on its executive committee met at a festive pre–Christmas dinner in the third-floor ballroom of B. F. Wilson's home on High Street (now Sixth Avenue).

Christmas cheer glowed in the red and green decorations —the red serving plates on the crescent-shaped table, the Christmas tree and other greenery inside the crescent, the red silk shades around the candles in the silver candelabra, the red carnations in silver bowls.

Each of the twenty-two men proposed toasts—all of them touching somehow on the Centennial. They remembered the last fireworks, the last concert, the final silence, the lights going out for the last time. But they also remembered the railroad—the inspiration for the whole thing.

J. W. Thomas, who had been president of the Centennial and president of the N. C. & St. L., offered a toast that summed up all their hope and confidence of growth.

"Every time I see a locomotive on its way," he said, lifting his glass high over the glowing assemblage, "I feel like throwing my hat into the air and shouting, 'Go on! Go on, civilizer of the world!'"

Nobody there would have seen anything strange about a Parthenon so near the railroad tracks.

Wilted Roses
versus Woman's Vote

The heavy fragrance of roses wilting on perspiring bosoms filled the caucus rooms at the Hotel Hermitage in the sweltering August of 1920, when the nation's leaders for and against woman's vote gathered for the showdown fight in Nashville.

Both sides made their headquarters at the Hermitage, then the city's ultimate in luxury hotels. Both sides identified themselves by the roses they wore: yellow for the Suffragists; red for the "Antis," those women and their backers fighting woman's vote.

The story of the women who won that battle and gave the right to vote to all American women has often been written. But now for the first time comes the story of Miss Josephine Pearson, the Tennessee-born and bred woman who became a power in the national fight opposed to woman's vote.

Now, for the first time, through a collection of her memoirs, speeches, and other papers in the Manuscript Division of the State Library and Archives, the quaint battle of women against woman's rights comes to light.

In the first place, it was one of the hottest Augusts that she could remember, Miss Pearson wrote. And in that era before air conditioning, the best that the corseted ladies could do was find a spot near electric fans.

Mrs. Carrie Chapman Catt, who came down from New York to lead the national suffragist group, suffered so from the humid days that she kept writing home for more clothes. Installed in her room on one of the upper floors of the hotel, she chose to keep herself in the background, not offending Tennessee legislators by "outside" pressure.

But swarming about the lobby, dining rooms, campaign headquarters, and elevators were scores of women from all over the United States, here to lobby either for or against woman's vote. Nashville ladies who had been good friends pretended not to see each other if they wore different-colored roses.

But this was no garden party. Politicians and big business interests from all over the nation threw their power into the fracas. Managing women's votes would be an unwieldy task, antisuffragist leaders figured. Men's votes could often be influenced through pressure on their jobs. But who could tell how a woman would vote?

Newspaper reporters from New York, Washington, Boston, Baltimore, and Chicago settled down at the Hermitage for weeks of reporting the final suffrage fight. Thirty-five states had already ratified the suffrage amendment. If Tennessee did so, that would make it national law. Tennessee legislators, battered with attentions from the warring women, could hardly push their way through the hotel lobby.

The several groups of women in Tennessee opposed to woman's vote had already merged for battle and had "drafted" Miss Pearson as their president. In that role, she directed the national "Anti" forces in Nashville. Insignia of her rank was the cluster of three red roses she wore, and no three-star general ever wore his stars more proudly.

Wherever she went in Nashville, Miss Pearson wrote, people recognized her three-rose rank. Practically every man and woman in Nashville wore either a red or a yellow rose to show which side he or she was on, and when Miss Pearson slipped out of her hotel headquarters early one morning to make a purchase in a lady's shop nearby, she was enchanted to see every saleslady there wearing a red rose.

A melodramatic woman, swathed in Victorian sentimentality, she wrote of herself as if she were the audience watching her own performance breathlessly. Emerging from a plump little pincushion of a world—all tufted and velvet and soft—she rose to new heights of oratorical power when she spoke to the Tennessee Senate and "seemed to hear my voice touch the Capitol Dome!"

Torn between her considerable power on the platform and the prim world that had taught her that ladies should not mix in the wicked world of politics, she wrote repeatedly that she "hated politics." Actually she grew up on politics, reading newspapers from all over the country and hearing the day's issues discussed morning, noon, and night in the home of her Methodist-minister father. It was a newspaper article, in fact, that set her on the antisuffragist campaign in Nashville.

Her reasons for fighting the right to vote are almost beyond understanding today. In a frenzy of emotionalism, she spoke of "preserving motherhood," as if the vote would somehow end that function. She wrote of keeping faith with the South and the Confederacy by denying women the vote. Her reasoning on that was that granting the right to vote was the state's prerogative. Other southern states had taken the "state's rights" position, and she thought Tennessee should stick by her sister southern states.

Another great fear of the Antis was that the black woman would be entitled to vote. It was bad enough to have black men voting, they argued. But to have a black woman come out of their kitchen and express her ideas at the polls was unthinkable.

In Nashville, *The Nashville Banner* and its hard-hitting

publisher, Maj. E. B. Stahlman, fought woman's suffrage. *The Nashville Tennessean,* published by Luke Lea, supported women in the fight for suffrage.

Newspapers like *The Grundy County Times* cited three "reasons" for opposing woman's vote: first, most women have work to do at home and should not have to take time off to vote; second, "motherhood is woman's business," and that leaves no time for a visit to the polls; third, men can represent women at the ballot box.

One of the magazines published in Washington, D.C., specifically to fight woman's vote was called *The Woman Patriot.* One of that paper's reasons for opposing the vote for women was that "The American Forestry Association estimates that over $100,000 worth of wood pulp and pencils will be wasted at the coming election on double suffrage." By depriving women of the right to vote, the government could save paper. What the editorial did not mention was how much could be saved by depriving all people of the right to vote.

To the Antis, there was nothing comic in the headline in a Nashville newspaper: "Shall the People or Women Rule?"

But Miss Pearson's blood boiled the day she picked up a Chattanooga newspaper and read that a suffragist speaker had accused Antis of being the tools of prostitutes and "the whisky element." As a child, Miss Pearson had ridden on Temperance floats through the streets of McMinnville, and her recitations on the evils of drink had wrenched the hearts of church congregations.

Her mother, the former Amanda Caroline Rascoe of Sumner County, had been a fierce Temperance leader for years and had fought equally hard against woman's vote. In fact, it was a promise that Josephine Pearson made to her mother, practically on her deathbed, that kept Miss Pearson fighting through the torrid 1920 suffrage campaign.

Born in Sumner County on June 30, 1868, on the farm of her great-grandfather, Alexander Rascoe I, Josephine Pearson was the daughter of a scholarly Methodist minister, P. A. Pearson, who taught and preached in Sumner County and in McMinnville. Miss Pearson's mother was a teacher of dramatics and "elocution" in the Old Liberty School in Sumner County for years, and her inventiveness (creating "ocean waves" by rippling sheets of tin across the stage, for instance) made her the artistic wonder of the community.

Miss Pearson, in her memoirs, wrote of her happy childhood as a performer in both church and school.

"As a child, I was much before the public in recitations and songs, many on the occasions for Temperance," she wrote. "As a small child, I well remember bowing at the knees of some incognito inebriate, singing out my little soul to the words, 'Please Do Not Leave Me Tonight, Dear Father!' until the entire audience wept!!!"

When Josephine Pearson was in high school in McMinnville, she had such firm political views that she stood up against her classmates and wore the red rose that admirers of Alf Taylor, Republican candidate for governor, wore in the hotly contested campaign of 1886.

Her Democratic classmates, horrified at first, came to admire her courage on that unpopular stand, she said. And then she finished college, majoring in philosophy, and went away to teach in colleges in Nashville, South Carolina, Memphis, Missouri, and Virginia.

She was dean of women at Christian College in Columbia, Missouri, when she began her study of the woman's suffrage issue, she said. She visited western states that had already granted women the right to vote, and she came away worried. She wrote articles for various publications, setting forth her strong feelings against women's votes.

"From 1909 to 1914, through my writing, I became a

leader of the 'Antis' in Missouri," Miss Pearson wrote.

In between her teaching, writing and speechmaking, she traveled over Europe, Mexico, Alaska, and Asia. And then, during commencement week of 1914 in Columbia, Missouri, she received a telegram from home that was to end her college teaching for years: her mother, living at Monteagle, had suffered a fall and was bedridden. Miss Pearson dropped everything to "rush to my mother's bedside."

For the next year she took care of her mother, until the latter died on July 12, 1915. A week before she died, Mrs. Pearson, sitting in the library of their Monteagle home, stopped Josephine one night before she left the room to retire. She demanded that forty-seven-year-old Josephine promise her that she would do all in her power to prevent woman's suffrage.

That "vow," taken with melodramatic flourishes, made the future campaigns a "holy war" to Josephine Pearson. She was obsessed with the idea of "keeping faith" with her mother.

"Only a few have known WHY [sic] the burden has been so a part of my life!" she recalled in a speech to her followers in September, 1920. "The consciousness of the sacred VOW to my sainted mother gave me a faith and courage to enter this last campaign in Tennessee! I have felt it to be a 'Holy War,' as it were. A crusade in memory of my Mother, for Southern Motherhood, in which her guiding spirit has lead me all the way!"

After her mother's death Miss Pearson not only plunged into a fury of writing articles and making speeches against woman's suffrage; she also devoted her time to caring for her aged father.

Life had settled down to a peaceful routine at their Monteagle home, called Stone Court, just inside the entrance gate to Monteagle Assembly Grounds. She and her father talked endlessly of presidential elections, the coming world war, and the threat of woman's suffrage as they read the daily *New York Times,* along with leading newspapers from Nashville, Chattanooga, and Memphis.

One summer morning in 1916, Miss Pearson strolled out the Assembly Grounds gate and across the tracks to the railway station, "in view of our house," to pick up her copy of *The Chattanooga Times.* She began skimming over the front page as she "slowly walked to my house, where sat on the veranda my father, waiting for the morning paper."

Her eyes fell on a story about a speech made by a woman suffragist at a Chattanooga convention, who said "that the Anti-Suffrage forces of America were allied with the Whiskey element and the Red Light Districts of America!"

Furious, Miss Pearson hurried to the porch to show the story to her father.

"I'm answering this challenge!" she announced. Her father begged her "not to enter a newspaper controversy." It was so unladylike, he said—"unthinkable for my daughter."

She went to her desk, dashed off her reply to that speech and got it on the 11 A.M. train for Chattanooga. Even her father agreed by that time that it was the honorable thing to do "in memory of my mother."

Her letter appeared in the next day's *Chattanooga Times,* and the world began changing rapidly for Miss Pearson. Telegrams from "leading Tennessee lawyers, both of the Democratic and Republican party leaders from New York to the Gulf," began pouring in, "assuring me their services and support."

And finally, after fiery exchanges in the newspapers, the Chattanooga speaker, Miss Ernestine Noe, apologized for her statement.

It was a cold day in January, 1917, when the state Association Opposed to Woman Suffrage invited Miss Pearson to Nashville. Mrs. John J. Vertrees, state president, and her husband, one of the most distinguished lawyers in the state, met Miss Pearson at Union Station. She was to be guest in their home and they had invited leading Nashville citizens in to meet her that night.

Upshot of that meeting was that the association unanimously "drafted" Miss Pearson as their next president. Before she accepted she consulted her father, who approved. And she consulted their old friend, Maj. E. C. Lewis, the Nashville railroad executive responsible for building the Parthenon replica in 1897 and Union Station in 1900. A peppery little man who made tough businessmen quake at his word, he in no way intimidated Miss Pearson.

"Mr. Vertrees drove me to see Major Lewis," Miss Pearson wrote. "I told him that I wished him to be a determining factor in my decision! His reply came promptly in the presence of Mr. Vertrees: 'Go to it, Dammit—and win!' "

The fact that Lewis's two daughters, Mrs. James S. Frazer and Mrs. Lytle Brown, were on the opposite side, fighting *for* woman's suffrage, made no difference to Lewis. And the fact that they had opposite views made no difference years later when Miss Pearson was ill and penniless, and Mrs. Frazer became her great benefactor.

Miss Pearson said she and the other Antis felt assured that the whole issue of woman's suffrage would be settled state by state—not by amendment to the federal constitution. President Woodrow Wilson, she said, had promised when he ran for office that he would support the "state's rights" approach.

But Tennessee women fighting for woman's suffrage, under the leadership of the capable Mrs. Guilford Dudley, had never let up in their campaign since they were organized in a quiet corner of the old Tulane Hotel on Wednesday morning, September 20, 1911. By 1915, news stories out of Washington were predicting that the powerful suffragist association in Tennessee might settle the national issue.

Yet it came as a "bolt from the blue," Miss Pearson said, when a telegram from President Wilson and a Tennessee senator stated "that for political expediency" Wilson would like to see Tennessee ratify the "federal suffrage bill."

The dramatic Miss Pearson enjoyed recounting the subsequent scenes: "I was at once rushed to the Vertrees residence. Scarcely had Mrs. Vertrees and myself finished reading the lines than Mr. Vertrees rushed home in his car.

"He said, 'Miss Pearson, you will send instructions to the Senate.' I said, 'Mr. Vertrees, I am going in person before the Senate!' "

With much gusto, Miss Pearson told of Vertrees' "masterful eloquence," when he reminded her of how "dignified" she had been in staying away from the Capitol. Vertrees begged her not to go, not to mar her record by mixing with politicians.

But Miss Pearson said the moment had come for action. She would go to the Senate. Vertrees said he would accompany her.

"If you go, you go as a lady, accompanied by a gentleman!" Vertrees commanded.

In silence they rode to the Capitol. Not until they mounted the steps to the senate room did Vertrees ask her what she was going to do. She confessed she had no idea.

"As one in a rage, I was led to the platform," she wrote. "I cannot remember the introduction, nor seemed to sense the sensation I was creating. The room was still as death!

"Then holding up that fatal telegram, I read it in a very ringing voice and concluded: 'Woodrow Wilson has overstepped the prerogative of the Office of the President of the United States! Will you submit to his dictatorship?' "

There was a great shout of approval, the Senate voted to kill the suffrage bill at that session, and Miss Pearson—

exhausted—rushed "home to the Mountain! To Peace! To the arms of an adoring father!"

Her father died in 1918, and by the summer of 1920 Miss Pearson had discovered that she must take in "paying guests" at her Monteagle home to pay off the mortgage. Her guests were only from the "very exclusive class," she said, as her "aristocratic mother" would have wished.

"I was in the midst of this venture, feeling very secure about the Legislature, when Gov. A. H. Roberts called the special session of the Legislature on July 17, 1920," she wrote.

Instantly Mrs. Carrie Chapman Catt, national leader in the fight for woman's suffrage, began moving her sizable forces into Nashville. And Mrs. Dudley had her well-organized Tennessee Suffragists ready for the fight.

The fight between Suffragists and the Antis settled down into a long, vicious, shrewdly fought campaign they called the "Verdun of 1920."

But on the steamy night of July 17, 1920, when Miss Pearson came down off her cool mountain to lay the battle plans, she was appalled by the city's heat. She asked for the cheapest room at the Hermitage for herself, and then engaged the assembly room on the mezzanine floor and the assembly room on the main floor as campaign headquarters for the Antis.

On that first night in her sticky little room, Miss Pearson suffered so from the heat that the only way she could endure it was to stand under the cool shower all night. As she stood in the tub, she composed telegrams to send out to Anti leaders throughout the nation.

"For hours I stood, wiring from my unmolested retreat, the messages to the East, South, even West," she wrote. "Came promptly the official assurance from New York and Boston—our forces en route."

The next day the national organization installed her in a

suitable room of her own on the northwest corner of the seventh floor—Room 718. Local social leaders, like Mrs. Van Leer Kirkman and Mrs. Leslie Warner, alongside Mrs. Dudley, gave prestige to the Suffragist side. On the other side, with Miss Pearson, were the imperious Mrs. George A. Washington of Washington Hall, along with the equally prominent Miss Josephine Farrell and Miss Mollie Claiborne.

Both sides saw to it that there were receptions, dinners, cooling drives through the countryside for visiting national leaders and legislators. And all of them buttonholed legislators in hotel lobby and dining room. But Miss Pearson announced from her seventh-floor aerie that the Antis would not stoop to go to Capitol Hill to talk to legislators.

When the legislators wanted to see the Antis, they were welcome to come to Anti headquarters at the Hermitage. But she kept her round-the-clock volunteers busy typing out press releases and bulletins to be left on the desk of every legislator before he turned up for work every morning. And she kept her private telephone line from her room going almost constantly.

As noses were counted and rumors of bribery published, Miss Pearson sometimes locked herself in Room 718 "for a spell" when she felt her temper about to explode.

The legislature had convened on August 9, 1920, and on the following Friday, August 13, the Senate voted for ratification of the suffrage amendment. But the House was so divided, seesawing first one way and then the other, that both sides were afraid to bring it to a vote.

Nevertheless speaker Seth Walker announced that a vote to table the amendment would be taken on Wednesday morning, August 18, and the ladies were up early to decorate the House with yellow and red roses. The halls and galleries were packed with women on both sides, glaring at each other as they crushed their roses in tight quarters.

But the Suffragists were whistling in the dark. In spite of their weeks of intensive work, all indications were that the vote would be forty-seven for the amendment and forty-nine against.

First break came when Rep. Banks Turner changed his mind and voted for woman's suffrage. That left the vote, on first roll call, deadlocked at forty-eight for and forty-eight against. But, on the third roll call, the fight was suddenly over. Harry Burn, youngest member of the legislature, changed his mind and broke the tie. At that moment, when the mountain youth voted for woman's suffrage, Tennessee gave the right to vote to all American women.

Miss Pearson, outraged at the turn of events, refused to believe Burn's story about the letter from his widowed mother that changed his vote. But the letter was there— with his mother at Niota reminding him that she, as a land-owner, had to pay taxes that her tenants voted for. The tenants, who had no land, imposed taxes on her, who had no vote.

The wrath of the Antis was so bitter that Burn barely escaped with his life. He was chased out of one of the third-floor windows of the Capitol and had to cling to a ledge to make his escape on the opposite side, to hide in the attic, under the hot roof.

For the next two days, various strategies were devised by the Antis to prevent the bill's coming up for a final vote, now that the tabling motion had failed.

Finally, on Friday, August 20, "in the dead of night," came the call to Miss Pearson in Room 718. She was to come secretly to Anti headquarters down on the mezzanine.

"Stealthily, by a side stair, I went from this high place to find our leaders in the Legislature were coralling our 27 men," Miss Pearson wrote of that midnight escapade. The plan was to get thirty-six legislators on the 3 A.M. train to

Alabama, and thus break the quorum the next morning.

"This Red Rose Brigade stayed in Alabama three weeks," Miss Pearson wrote proudly.

But the scheme did not work. Those legislators who were present for the Saturday morning, August 21, session decided that their vote against the tabling motion on Wednesday was tantamount to passing the suffrage bill. Not all of the protests from the absent legislators nor all of the parliamentary maneuvers tried in the next few weeks could change that.

Gov. A. H. Roberts signed the bill on the following Tuesday, August 24, and on August 26, with the president's signature, the bill became national law. Whistles blew, bells rang, victorious Suffragists paraded under showers of confetti on New York's Fifth Avenue.

Meanwhile Miss Pearson suffered disconsolately. She and her fellow Antis envisioned prolonged court battles, but before the Supreme Court could act on the matter, Connecticut became the thirty-seventh state to ratify, and fighting woman's suffrage was a dead issue.

"Tired and heart-sick to have fallen a victim of Perfidy, I never in all the years before or since have felt so empty a void in life," Miss Pearson wrote. "Lost Ideals! Not defeat, but disgrace from my native state."

She went "home to the Mountains" to recuperate from the long battle and in October resigned as president of the state antisuffrage association. Later, while she was teaching in a Virginia college, illness struck, and in 1930, at age sixty-two, she reluctantly retired.

Her last years, spent in the Old Woman's Home on West End Avenue, were tortured with pain. Her money was gone, and it was only through the generosity of the late Mrs. James S. Frazer that she was able to live in the comfort of that home.

But she never lost her flair for the dramatic—even writing at length about the details of her funeral. She wanted to be wrapped in a "winding sheet" and covered by a purple shawl that she had bought in Rome after days of walking through the hot Italian streets.

In the end, Miss Pearson—the proud, the imperious defender of Victorian myths (that men, for instance, should support women and do the voting for them)—had to face reality. She forgave old enemies who had defeated her in her attempts to deprive women of the vote.

And she had only one wish: to be buried between her parents, whom she adored, "under the pines of Monteagle." There she was buried after her death on November 3, 1944, at age seventy-six—a sad link with another century, another world.

All Aboard
for Union Station

The bright October morning in 1900 that Union Station was formally opened, a brisk wind whipped the flags flying in front, along each side of the Broad Street viaduct, as the Marine Band played and town leaders paraded by, on their way to the ceremony.

But the tension between speakers on the platform behind the station, where the program began at 10 A.M., was the culmination of years of feuding—well known to the audience packed and jammed below, at track level, under the huge train shed. Railroad had fought railroad for the privilege of using station facilities, and all of them had fought competing steamboats.

Not even the presence of the smiling ladies—the city's social leaders—who presided at the reception later in the rotunda, under the vaulted stained-glass ceiling sixty-three feet above, dulled the bite of speeches by Mayor James M. Head and others who resented the exclusion of one railroad from the station.

Newspapers had joined the fight.

"An epoch will this day be made for Nashville," *The Nashville American* bravely proclaimed in a front-page editorial that Tuesday morning, October 9, 1900. "The great stone edifice at Broad and Walnut Street is the matchless monument to record the fact. The epoch is one of larger progress and more persistent enterprise."

The mayor of Nashville and other speakers on the land-

186

ing of the central stairway leading down to the tracks raised the question: Would Nashville indeed forge ahead as a shipping center? Or would the warring railroads fight each other so viciously that they would lose to the steamboat competition?

Certainly nobody there gave a thought to the possibility that the automobile—nothing but a sportsman's toy then— would bring doom to both riverboat and railroad.

The day the massive stone building with its great square tower rose above the Broad Street viaduct like a gawky giant, it seemed sure to dominate the future.

But today the giant is old and ailing. At present the roof leaks. The tile floors swim in dirty puddles when it rains. The long, custom-made benches were long ago pushed out of the rain and stored elsewhere. The row of ticket windows where travelers used to stand in line for tickets to New York or New Orleans, Chicago or Chattanooga, has been boarded up for years.

The doors at the Broad Street entrance have long been locked. The cold, dank air that grips the empty waiting room has yet the smell of ancient disinfectant, of smoke long abolished in favor of diesel fuel, of an era almost as extinct as the era of stagecoaches.

In its last active days, when only two trains a day passed through—one going north to Chicago and the other south to Florida—the few passengers boarding those trains waited for hours in a tight little corner improvised in what was once the Ladies Waiting Room. There was no gloomier spot in Nashville.

One former railroad executive stepped inside the station on a rainy afternoon just before the station closed in 1975 to have a final look, and at first glance he saw nothing but the rain pouring from the ceiling high above. The splash of water on tile-bottomed puddles was all he heard.

"Then I looked through the shadows and saw one man

sitting on one of the old benches," the railroad man said.

"Finally I recognized him. He was one of my old railroad friends, stopping for a look. When I spoke to him, he was startled.

" 'I thought I was dead,' he said. 'I thought we were all dead.' "

But there are thousands of Nashvillians very much alive to the value of the unique and still-strong building, and full of energy to try to revive it for a useful life for years to come. Long listed on the National Register of Historic Places, the building was selected in 1978 as the first historic railroad station in the nation to be restored through the General Services Administration. That same year Congress voted $7.1 million for the project and had hoped to have the work well under way in time to celebrate the city's 200th birthday in 1980. So far, the work of eradicating damage done by pigeons loose in the deserted building has postponed all other efforts.

Architects marvel at the station's lofty interior construction and the well-preserved stained glass, wrought iron, plaster detail, and stonework still shouting of the grandeur of its era. Its fanciful roofline and tall tower speak loudly of Nashville's grasp at commercial expansion as no other building can.

The personalities who shaped that building, the bitter feuds that culminated in that proud tower, the battle for trade between steamboats and railroads and the equally bitter battle among the railroads themselves helped shape the businesses that thrive in Nashville today.

On that sunny October morning when crowds packed the three long flights of steps to hear speakers of the day, the genial Maj. John W. Thomas, much-loved citizen and president of the Nashville, Chattanooga & St. Louis Railway, reminded them that the railroads had been planning a Union Station for twenty-eight years.

There had been half a dozen small stations in Nashville, each serving short lines. Some of the small lines had been bought by larger lines and absorbed by either the Louisville & Nashville Railroad or the N. C. & St. L.

In 1872, he told them, the railroads had planned to build their station on Church Street, and then in 1884 they decided to build on Broad Street. But the N. C. & St. L. could not swing the deal alone, he said. It was only after the L&N made the money available through its board chairman, New York tycoon August Belmont, that work could begin on the mammoth station.

And there many hearts sank.

The giant railroad with roots in the North would gobble up the South's own N. C. & St. L.

Mayor Head, a handsome, scholarly lawyer and former newspaperman, pulled no punches when it came his turn to welcome Mr. Belmont and other investors in the new terminal station.

It seemed to him, he said, that if it were truly a Union Station or a Terminal Station it would permit all trains through Nashville to use its facilities. As it was, of course, only the L&N and the N. C. & St. L. had that privilege.

"Let us hope that these public-spirited men who have put their money in this enterprise will be big enough and broad enough and bold enough to come to look upon Nashville not as a lemon to be squeezed, nor even as a rich harvest to be gathered," Head said, "but as a fertile field to be cared for and cultivated, out of which untold wealth may continue to be garnered in all the years to come."

Mayor Head was a close friend of Jere Baxter, who was furious because his railroad, the Tennessee Central, had been denied use of the new station. Partly because of the wrath brought down upon him by these brash words, Head soon left Nashville forever and practiced law in Boston, the city he had come to love when he was a student at Harvard.

But the men on the speaker's platform that opening day at Union station were aware of greater struggles than that.

For the story of Union Station reached back to stage-coach days, when railroads first promised to go to markets no riverboat could touch.

By threading their way through the hills and across the vast flatlands of Tennessee, the rails were to shape the social life of every community where trains stopped. They were to determine battle lines during the Civil War. They were to weave industry and jobs and colleges and families together in countless new ways and—on both national and state levels—the rails would slither ruthlessly through political life for half a century before Union Station was built.

Straddling the two centuries precisely, railroads in Nashville had fifty years planted firmly in the 1800s and fifty years in the 1900s, and Union Station rose exactly at the dividing line between the two.

The first fifty years were seared with disappointment and setbacks—with fortunes lost in the effort, and treachery from northern speculators and local politicians.

And they had hardly got their trains on the tracks when the Civil War left the railroads bankrupt. Floods and washed-out bridges, bad crops and epidemics of yellow fever and cholera cut severely into the dreams.

The second fifty years captured the excitement—and profit—of railroading in her heyday. It was an era when Nashville railroads counted their passengers by the millions and unloaded freight cars on the crowded tracks around the clock.

Andrew Jackson was still living at the Hermitage when the Nashville and Chattanooga Railway was in the planning stage, in 1843. Jackson died on June 8, 1845, and on December 11 of that same year the N & C received her charter.

The plans were to build a track from Nashville to Chattanooga, and thus serve as a connecting link between trains running to the port city of Charleston, South Carolina, on the east and St. Louis and more distant markets to the west.

V. K. Stevenson, Nashville businessman who was later to serve as president of the Nashville and Chattanooga, wrote the famous statesman John C. Calhoun to try to persuade South Carolinians that they would profit by helping build the N & C.

On December 12, 1846, Stevenson wrote Calhoun about the wide variety of Tennessee products that could be shipped yearly through the Charleston port if the N & C could be built.

Among Tennessee's products, Stevenson said, were not only manufactured goods but also "23,000 gallons of peach and apple brandy at 60 cents a gallon; 15,000 barrels of whiskey at $8.00 per barrel, made chiefly at Nashville," and vast amounts of "wheat, wool, cotton, tobacco, hogs, cattle, etc."

Charleston promptly subscribed $500,000 toward building the N & C, and Atlanta and Augusta and Murfreesboro subscribed smaller amounts.

Confident Middle Tennesseans were soon assuring doubting citizens that they could get past the hurdle of the Cumberland Mountains by "boring a hole through it."

That was, in fact, the first task that the new railroad set for itself. In March, 1848, the enormous job of hacking a tunnel through 2,200 feet of solid rock, by hand labor, began.

With white and slave labor, with sledgehammers, hand drills, black powder and pick shovels, the tunnel was built in four years. Beginning at both ends and working toward the middle, 170 feet below the top of the mountain, the men lighted their way with smoking torches.

Meantime, the tracks were being laid and the bridges built, and on December 30, 1850, the first locomotive, the Tennessee, arrived in Nashville on the steamboat *Beauty.*

Some of the rails and other equipment were made in England and shipped to Nashville by river, through New Orleans. But the "locomotive, tender, 13 freight cars and a splendid passenger car" were made in Cincinnati, and they too arrived on the *Beauty*.

They were all unloaded at the Broad Street wharf and pulled by mule power to newly laid tracks nearby, and on December 28, 1850, *The True Whig* reported that Nashville's first locomotive had made its first trial run—one mile out on the N & C tracks.

"It marked an era in our history," the newspaper announced proudly.

After overwhelming setbacks from weather and epidemics and steamboat competition, the railroads in Nashville were just beginning to make a profit when the Civil War brought combat to Nashville's doorstep.

The N & C station stood at Tenth and Church Street then, near the east end of what is now the Church Street viaduct. The Union Army, after capturing Nashville in February, 1862, confiscated the railway facilities and operated them throughout the war.

Union troops by the thousands and materiel by the trainload passed through the crowded Church Street station, and finally, on December 15, 1864, the struggle for possession of the prized transportation systems brought on the Battle of Nashville, disastrous for the South.

The defeat at Nashville was, some historians say, decisive in the defeat of the whole Confederacy.

Even when the battle was over and the war was ended, Federal forces continued to hold Nashville under their military control. And two years after the war was over, when the Federal government began to negotiate return of the railroad to its owners, the latter were aghast.

They found the railroad in "deplorable condition, verging on bankruptcy," a later president of the railroad, the late W. S. Hackworth, wrote in 1953, in *Over a Century of Railroad Service.*

The railroad was "without rolling stock to operate it, without machine shops or machinery . . . the road in bad order, the bridges worn out and unsafe, the station houses destroyed, or those still standing unfit for use, without a dollar in the treasury to commence operations, with a floating debt of between $600,000 and $700,000 . . . without books or stationery."

But the worst was yet to come.

The Federal government said they had spent $1.5 million on equipment and improvements, and they would return the wrecked railroad to its owners only if the latter guaranteed repayment of that amount in monthly payments, at the then-exorbitant interest rate of 7.3 percent.

N & C owners had no choice. They agreed to the government terms, and then had to borrow money from private lenders at 4 percent interest to meet government demands.

They did finally pay off the debt, and were at the same time pushing hard to get out of their tiny, outmoded brick station on Church Street and build one of the lofty train stations like those rising in big cities across the land.

Their plan to extend their line to St. Louis became a reality in 1880, when they bought a short connecting line, and they operated it for six months. In anticipation of that event, they had changed their name in 1873 to Nashville, Chattanooga & St. Louis.

But the mighty Louisville and Nashville Railroad, with headquarters in Louisville and controlling ownership in New York, cut that dangerously competitive operation off almost before it got started.

The L&N bought controlling stock in the N. C. & St. L. and then sold the latter's newly acquired St. Louis branch to the L&N.

Nashville businessmen were furious at the maneuver.

From then on, some railroad men said, the N. C. & St. L. worked under a shadow—the threat that the L&N would someday take them over.

When the L&N did indeed bring in the money to build the new Union Station, the company infuriated many Nash-villians by cutting a deep gulch through the rocky hillside on Broad Street and turning what had been a fashionably residential area into a commercial center.

The N. C. & St. L. hoped to have the new Union Station built in time for the Centennial celebration of 1897, and, in fact, the same men were responsible for both the Centennial and the station.

The railroad's purpose in staging the Centennial celebration was of course to bring thousands of visitors to Nashville by train, and to publicize the commercial opportunities in a city prepared to ship by railroad to many parts of the country.

Major Thomas, president of the N. C. & St. L., was also president of the Centennial celebration. Major Lewis, who as director general of the Centennial had made it the most successful grand exposition in the history of the country, was also made chief planner of the new Union Station.

The two railroads, the L&N and the N. C. & St. L., formed a third company, the Nashville Terminal Company, to be responsible for building the new Union Station on Broad Street. They made Lewis president of the terminal company.

It was Lewis who had planned the Parthenon as symbol of Nashville's reputation as the "Athens of the South."

A peppery little man, a perfectionist who planned every detail in the enormously successful Centennial, Lewis went after the Union Station project with the same precision.

He had bought a newspaper, *The Nashville American,* to publicize the Centennial, and he used it to promote the controversial Union Station. For ten years the railroad had dickered with Nashville's city council to get permission to build on the Broad Street site, and it was actually Lewis who was determined that the new building would excite the city to a new commercial growth.

As 200 homes and other buildings were destroyed to make way for the fifty-seven acres needed for the new Union Station and its tracks, many Nashvillians moved to the suburbs in a huff.

Residents in the Broad Street area were further offended when the railroad built Cummins Station, a storage area behind Union Station. That was to compete with the riverboats, with their storage facilities near the river, offering convenience to their shippers.

But Lewis's paper hammered away at the new life the Union Station would bring to the city's commerce, and he saw to it that the tower, including the 20-foot figure of Mercury on top, rose to a height of 239 feet.

He had removed Mercury, Greek god of commerce, from atop the Commerce Building on the Centennial grounds when that celebration was over, and he doubtless had a hand in planning symbolic female figures hovering over the arches above the balconies overlooking the deep well of the station's waiting room.

Those plaster figures, holding Tennessee products including wheat, corn, tobacco, and whiskey, had their human duplicates on opening day, when Lewis had girls from Ward's Seminary, "dressed in white, representing the ministerial angels of commerce," take part in the program.

As "ladies bountiful," the schoolgirls, sitting on the stage, "tripped forward, one at a time, depositing products of the state," *The Nashville American* reported.

Frances McLester brought hops, and Sara Sperry brought a piece of lumber. Lizzie Nichol brought tobacco, and Mattie Nichol brought coal.

And August Belmont, true to his habit of not speaking in public, simply made a deep bow to the audience.

Union Station was certainly not the first tower on Broad Street. The handsome gray Gothic Federal Building at Seventh and Broad had its cornerstone laid by President Rutherford B. Hayes in September, 1877, and First Baptist Church, across the street at Seventh and Broad, dedicated its Victorian red brick church with the pointed steeple and tower (preserved in the new building on the same site) in 1886.

But it was the custom of railroads then to build tall towers with clocks in them, to impress travelers with the punctuality of their trains. And it was Lewis's idea, almost his obsession, to have the four digital clocks on the four sides of the tower so accurate that any businessman could set his watch by them. His own collection of clocks, in his home, had to be synchronized to sound off at precisely the same moment when he arrived home every day, or there was woe to his household, members of his family said.

But Lewis was not the architect of Union Station. He had, working under his direction, an Irish-born engineer-architect, Richard Montfort, who had designed bridges for the L&N for twenty years before he drew up plans for Union Station. He picked up ideas from massive public buildings in Pennsylvania and from railway stations in Chicago and St. Louis.

But it was almost surely Lewis who designed a heating and cooling system for the station that was far ahead of its time. By that plan, the main floor of the station had under it a five-foot-deep space between it and the basement ceiling.

In that tightly insulated space, air was drawn down from the chimney tower (at the back of the buildings), was drawn across steam-heated coils for warming, and was circulated by fans to all floors of the station, through a network of ventilators.

In warm weather the heat was cut off, but the fans under

the floor kept fresh air from the chimney circulating through the building. It was perhaps Nashville's first air-conditioned building. (Later, unfortunately, that heating and cooling system was abandoned in favor of steam heat. But much of the equipment for the original system is still there—except for the fans.)

Lewis, conferring with architect and engineer, with stonemasons and clockmaker, with stained-glass makers and plumbers, with ironmongers and carpenters, cracked the whip to give the station a soaring touch of elegance.

The ponderous stone arches at the Broad Street entrance, the arched windows, the rows of arches above the balcony helped classify it as "Richardson Romanesque," popular in the late 1890s.

The cut Bowling Green stone with carved granite and Tennessee marble trim, the skylight that pours sunlight through the stained-glass panels in the arched ceiling, the rhythm of the roof line broken by ornamental dormers, the grouping of arched windows on two floors and squared-off windows in between make for a certain symmetry.

But it was the ceiling, reaching three stories above the waiting room, with balconies all around, that took the visitor's breath away.

For college students, mounting the long flights of steps from track level to begin Christmas vacation at home was always an exciting moment.

For a young country boy, Douglas Peacher, who had sold a pig to buy his ticket to Nashville and his first job, that stairway to the lofty Union Station was inspiration for the great adventure ahead.

As head of Sears in Canada and as retired Marine Corps officer, General Peacher said he never forgot the exhilaration of that moment.

For Dr. Merrill Moore, Boston psychiatrist-poet who grew up in Nashville and was graduated from Vanderbilt, the memory of the hissing and puffing of steam from the great locomotives when he was a three-year-old stayed with him all of his life. Terrified by the sound and the sight of it all, he clung to his mother's skirts and later drew on the experience to write his best-known poem, "The Noise That Time Makes."

There were ten tracks for passenger trains running under the giant shed, and for years the clamor of distant whistles and near bells, of shouting conductors and running porters, of locomotives chugging slowly out from under the great, shadowy, enormously romantic shed was excitement distilled.

Commuters by the thousands traveled by "accommodation trains," making the round trip daily to Nashville from Dickson, Columbia, Murfreesboro, and dozens of other Middle Tennessee towns.

Romance blossomed on the commuter trains, and conductors, who knew who was courting whom, gave the young couples as much time as possible to say their farewells on the platform before boarding the train.

During World War I, when thousands commuted daily to Old Hickory to work in Dupont's powder plant, there were special trains making the round trip at every shift, and eight or ten cars in every train.

Patriotic young ladies by the hundreds rode the commuter trains to Old Hickory every day to do their stint in the factory, and their trains, called the Ladies Trains, were peaceful retreats for knitting and reading on the way to and from work.

Mrs. Sam Doak of Nashville remembers the vacation trips to visit relatives in Chattanooga, when packing the shoebox lunch for the long train trip was part of the excitement. The lunch usually included fried chicken and sandwiches, cake and fresh fruit, like peaches.

"We children always had our 'eating aprons,' made of

brown domestic with decorative edging, to wear over our nice clothes while eating our box lunch on the train," Mrs. Doak said.

When her aunt came from Chattanooga for a month's visit in the summertime, she always packed a damp sponge with the lunch box.

"That was to hold over her nose when they passed through the tunnel, to keep the cinders out of her nose and mouth," Mrs. Doak said.

In World War I, when thousands of soldiers and civilians died in the influenza epidemic, trainloads of caskets waited alongside the tracks to be shipped in or out for burial.

Morris Mashburn of Nashville, a former N. C. & St. L. executive, said he remembered the stacks of caskets, one on top of the other, reaching all the way down the platform, for perhaps 200 feet.

"It was a sight I will never forget—by far the saddest I have ever seen," Mashburn said.

There were tearful farewells at all seasons, but those during World War I and World War II were the most poignant. Red Cross canteens were set up beside the tracks, and soldiers passing through the station by the trainload had a chance at free refreshments and conversations with public-spirited hostesses.

And railroad men remember the long trains of German prisoners of war staring curiously as they passed through the station. They never forget the flag-draped coffins, arriving after each campaign, with military escorts standing at attention.

But about the time air conditioning took the cinders out of train travel, automobiles began to make the whole scene look obsolete.

By the time, in 1953, that the N. C. & St. L. had replaced all its old coal-fired locomotives with new diesel engines and cleaned a half-century of smoke off the blackened

Union Station, people weren't going there any more.

Trucks could haul much of the freight, and freight was what made the difference between profit and loss. As one trainman wrote in a poem about the glamorous train of long ago, *The Dixie Flyer,* "Dixie was a lady ... But it is the freight train—dirty hogger—There's the bloke responsible for bringing on payday."

To pamper passengers coming up from the tracks to the waiting room, an escalator was installed in 1948. But there were few passengers to use it. In 1950, all commuter trains and most of the twenty-two regular passenger trains a day were gone.

And then, almost symbolically, in a storm in 1953, the tall statue of Mercury toppled from its tower and crashed on the tracks below.

Four years later, the final blow came. The L&N took over the N. C. & St. L. completely, moved all administrative offices to Louisville, and left the almost empty ghost of a building to gather cobwebs in her lofty corners.

But architects, engineers, and businessmen judge the building too valuable to lose, and experts in restoration believe it can be put to good use again as a center for offices and shops.

The General Services Administration has had teams of exterminators in the building intermittently for more than a year, trying to rid the station of disease-bearing material left by pigeons. Still sheathed in scaffolding for the pigeon battle, the building stands in neglect, victim of a delay in federal funds. But there is some indication now that pressure from the Metropolitan Historical Commission, Nashville's mayor, Tennessee's two senators, and Nashville's congressman may soon see the renovation project through.

As Major Lewis said on opening day at Union Station in 1900, "The station has a thousand tongues." It is just a matter of who is listening.

Bibliography

Gen. Francis Nash Gave the City His Name

Ashe, Samuel A. *Biographical History of North Carolina, from Colonial Times to the Present.* Greensboro, N.C.: C. L. Van Noppen, 1905.

Blackwelder, Ruth. *The Age of Orange, Political and Intellectual Leadership in North Carolina, 1752–1861.* Charlotte, N.C.: William Loftin, Publisher, 1961.

Burke, Thomas. Letter to Governor Caswell, July 5, 1777, from Philadelphia. Library, University of North Carolina, Chapel Hill.

Cameron, Annie Sutton. *Hillsborough and the Regulators.* Hillsborough, N.C.: Orange County Museum, 1962.

Caswell, Gov. R. Letter to Captain William Caswell from New Bern, N.C., November 11, 1777. University of North Carolina, Chapel Hill.

Engstrom, Mary Claire. "William Hooper's Hillsborough Years, 1782–1790." *Daughters of the American Revolution Magazine,* February, 1974.

———. "School Lives in Memory of Hillsboro Residents." *Durham Morning Herald,* February 16, 1964.

Henderson, Archibald. "Abner Nash, Native of Virginia, Gave Life of Service to State." Unidentified newspaper story. Orange County Public Library, Hillsborough, N.C.

Historic American Buildings Survey. The Nash-Hooper House, 118 West Tryon Street, Hillsborough, N.C.

Laws of North Carolina, 1784, pp. 616–17, Chapter XLVII. Orange County Court House, Hillsborough, N.C.

Nash, Francis. Letters. Southern Historical Collection, University of North Carolina Library, Chapel Hill, N.C.

Nash, Francis. *Hillsboro, Colonial and Revolutionary.* Raleigh, N.C.: Edwards & Broughton printers, 1903.

———. *Historic Hillsboro.* Raleigh, N.C.: E. M. Uzzell & Co., printers, 1903.

North Carolina State Records. Orange County Court Records, Hillsboro, N.C., pp. 115–21; 278–79; 650–51; 789–90.

Orange County Court Records, 1764. Francis Nash, county clerk, charged with overcharging on court fee.

Ramsey, James G. M. *Annals of Tennessee.* Charleston: Walker & James, 1853.

Sanford, Cecil, Jr. Owner of Francis Nash home, Hillsborough, N.C. Interview by author, 1977.

Waddell, Alfred Moore. "General Francis Nash." Speech delivered at Guilford Battle Ground, 1906. North Carolina State Library, Raleigh.

Gen. William Lee Davidson, "Completely Adored"

Gen. William Lee Davidson, "Winner of Men"

Clayton, W. Woodford. *History of Davidson County, Tennessee.* Philadelphia: J. W. Lewis & Co., 1880.

Davidson, Chalmers G. *Piedmont Partisan, The Life and Times of General William Lee Davidson.* Davidson, N.C.: Davidson College, 1951.

———. *The Plantation World Around Davidson,* 2d ed. rev. Davidson, N.C.: The Mecklenburg Historical Association, 1973.

———. "Generals William Lee Davidson and Francis Nash." Speech Given to Tennessee Historical Society, May 10, 1976.

McLean family genealogical data, 1730–1819. Tennessee Historical Society, Tennessee State Library and Archives, Nashville.

Petition filed in Third Auditor's Office for Children of William Lee Davidson. Senate and House of Representatives of the United States. 1791.

Thomas, Jane H. *Old Days in Nashville.* Nashville: Publishing House Methodist Episcopal Church, South, Barbee & Smith, Agents, 1897.

Williamson, Hugh. Letter to Richard Bland Lee about William Lee Davidson, written from New York, May 19, 1810. Collection of Chalmers G. Davidson, Davidson College.

James Robertson, Founder of Nashville

Cotten, John. "The Battle of the Bluffs" from the *Journal of John Cotten.* Edited by J. W. L. Matlock. *Tennessee Historical Quarterly,* September, 1959.

Kelley, Sarah Foster. *Children of Nashville.* Nashville: Blue & Gray Press, 1973.

Matthews, Thomas Edwin. *General James Robertson, Father of Tennessee.* Nashville: The Parthenon Press, 1934.

———. Papers, 1789–1945. Manuscript Section, Tennessee State Library and Archives.

Murdock Collection. Overton Papers, 1780–1851, including letters to Robertson. Manuscript Section, Tennessee State Library and Archives.

Putnam, Albigence W. *History of Middle Tennessee, or Life and Times of General James Robertson.* 1859. Reprint. Knoxville, Tenn.: University of Tennessee Press, 1971.

Robertson, James. Papers and correspondence, including letter to John Sevier, governor of State of Franklin, 1787; to sons Peyton and John McNairy Robertson in 1834; to George M. Deaderick in 1811. Manuscript Section, Tennessee State Library and Archives.

Indian Fighter John Rains in "This Perilous Wilderness"

Clayton, W. Woodford. *History of Davidson County, Tennessee.* Philadelphia: J. W. Lewis & Co., 1880.

Cotten, John. "The Battle of the Bluffs" from the *Journal of John Cotten.* Edited by J. W. L. Matlock. *Tennessee Historical Quarterly,* September, 1959.

Davis, John. Letter to Lyman C. Draper on Nickajack campaign. Draper Collection. Manuscript Section, Tennessee State Library and Archives.

Deeds. Davidson County Register's Office. Land bought by John Rains listed in many purchases from 1786 to 1834. Davidson County Court House, Nashville.

Goodpasture, Albert W. "Indian Wars and Warriors of the Old Southwest, 1830–1837." *Tennessee Historical Magazine,* June, 1918.

Horn, Stanley F. Interview by author about former Rains home, 1977.

Land Grants from North Carolina, from 1786 to 1827, in Davidson, Sumner, Cocke, and Bledsoe counties. Manuscript Section, Tennessee State Library and Archives.

Putnam, Albigence W. *History of Middle Tennessee, or Life and Times of General James Robertson.* 1859. Reprinted. Knoxville, Tenn.: University of Tennessee Press, 1971.

Rains, John. Will, November 16, 1835. Davidson County. Manuscript Section, Tennessee State Library and Archives.

———. Division of Personal Estate, recorded July 16, 1835, Nashville. Manuscript Section, State Library and Archives.

Rains, Jonathan H. Sketch of Capt. John Rains by his son. Draper Collection. Manuscript Section, Tennessee State Library and Archives.

Dr. John Shelby's Christmas Present

Anderson, James Douglas. *Making the American Thoroughbred.* Norwood, Mass.: The Plimpton Press, 1916.

Cisco, Jay Guy. *Historic Sumner County.* Nashville: Folk-Keelin Printing Co., 1909.

Clayton, W. Woodford. *History of Davidson County, Tennessee.* Philadelphia: J. W. Lewis & Co., 1880.

Deeds. John Shelby Property. Davidson County Register's Office, Nashville.

Durham, Walter T. *Old Sumner, A History of Sumner County from 1805 to 1861.* Nashville: The Parthenon Press, 1972.

Frank, John G. "Adolphus Heiman." *Tennessee Historical Society Quarterly,* March, 1946.

Guild, Jo C. *Old Times in Middle Tennessee.* Nashville: Tavel, Eastman & Howell, printers, 1878.

Ikenberry, Margaret M. "Dr. John Shelby." In *Send For A Doctor.* Nashville: Public Library of Nashville and Davidson County, 1975.

Lindsley, John Berrien. Family papers. Diaries mentioning persons eminent in church, educational, medical, and political circles of Nashville from 1840 to 1866. Manuscript Section, Tennessee State Library and Archives.

McGavock, Randal. *Pen and Sword, the Life and Journals of Randal W. McGavock.* Edited by Herschel Gower and Jack Allen. Jackson, Tenn.: The Tennessee Historical Commission, 1960.

Murdock Collection. Overton Papers, 1780–1851, correspondence of Judge John Overton. Manuscript Section, Tennessee State Library and Archives.

Proceedings of Medical Society of Tennessee 1830–1844. Manuscript Section, Tennessee State Library and Archives.

Shelby, Dr. John. Collection of letters. Manuscript Section, Tennessee State Library and Archives.

George Deaderick, Banker in Knee Pants

Clayton, W. W. *History of Davidson County, Tennessee.* Philadelphia: J. W. Lewis & Co., 1880.

Deaderick, Mrs. Adeline. "Civil War Memories." Edited by Anna Mary Moon. *Tennessee Historical Quarterly,* March, 1948.

Deaderick, George M. Will recorded March 22, 1817. Manuscript Section, Tennessee State Library and Archives.

Deeds. Davidson County Register's Office. Lots and farms bought by George M. Deaderick from 1788 to 1816.

Jackson, Andrew. Letters from George M. Deaderick to Andrew Jackson, from 1799 to 1815. Jackson Papers. The Hermitage, Nashville.

James, Marquis. *The Life of Andrew Jackson.* New York: The Bobbs-Merrill Company, 1938.

Moon, Anna M. "Sketches of Shelby, McDowell, Deaderick Families." Manuscript Section, Tennessee State Library and Archives.

Murdock Collection. Overton Papers, 1780–1851. Letter to Deaderick, 1799. Manuscript Section, Tennessee State Library and Archives.

Overton, John. Letter. Claybrooke and Overton Papers. Manuscript Section, Tennessee State Library and Archives.

Thomas, Jane H. *Old Days in Nashville.* Nashville: Publishing House Methodist Episcopal Church, South, Barbee & Smith, Agents, 1897.

Earthquake Opens "Fountain of Health"

Armes, Ethel. *Stratford Hall.* Richmond, Va.: Garrett and Massie, 1936.

Clarion and Tennessee Gazette. Nashville. July 13, 1813.

Democratic Gazette and Clarion. Nashville. December 16, 1811.

Fuller, M. L. "The New Madrid Earthquake." *U.S. Geological Survey Bulletin 494,* 1912.

Hailey, Syd Houston. Interview by author about family deeds, wills, records of his wife's great-grandfather, William Saunders Sr., owner of Fountain of Health, Nashville, 1968.

James, Marquis. *The Life of Andrew Jackson.* New York: The Bobbs-Merrill Company, 1938.

Moneymaker, Berlen C. "Early Earthquakes in Tennessee and Adjacent States (1699 to 1850)." *Journal of the Tennessee Academy of Science,* vol. 29, no. 3, July, 1954.

Weakley, Sam A. Interview by author about deeds to land where Fountain of Health stood, 1968. Also survey of roads leading to Fountain.

Partying in Nashville in 1827

Clayton, W. *History of Davidson County, Tennessee.* Philadelphia: J. W. Lewis & Co., 1880.

Conner, Juliana Margaret. Diary from June 10 to October 17, 1827. Manuscript Section, Tennessee State Library and Archives.

Davidson, Chalmers G. *The Plantation World around Davidson.* Davidson, N.C.: Davidson Printing Company, 1973.

McGavock, Randal. *Pen and Sword, the Life and Journals of Randal W. McGavock.* Edited by Herschel Gower and Jack Allen. Jackson, Tenn.: The Tennessee Historical Commission, 1960.

William Strickland, Capitol Architect
Strickland's Triumph in Marble and Bronze

Capitol and Strickland Papers. Archives Division, Tennessee State Library and Archives.

Clayton, W. W. *History of Davidson County, Tennessee.* Philadelphia: J. W. Lewis & Co., 1880.

Dekle, Clayton B. "The Tennessee State Capitol." *Tennessee Historical Quarterly,* vol. XXV, no. 3, fall, 1966.

Gilchrist, Agnes Eleanor. *William Strickland, Architect and Engineer, 1788–1854.* Philadelphia: University of Pennsylvania Press, 1950.

Mahoney, Nell Savage. "William Strickland and the Building of Tennessee's Capitol, 1845–1854." *Tennessee Historical Quarterly,* vol. IV, no. 2, June, 1945.

———. "William Strickland's Introduction to Nashville." *Tennessee Historical Quarterly,* vol. IX, no. 1, March 1950.

Strickland, William. *Reports on Canals, Railways, Roads and Other Subjects.* Philadelphia: Pennsylvania Society for the Promotion of Internal Improvement, 1826.

———. *Sketches of Roman Architecture.* Philadelphia. 1838.

When Cholera Laid Our City Low

Chambers, Dr. J. S. *The Conquest of Cholera.* New York: MacMillan, 1938.

Cholera statistics from 1831 to 1870. Reference Room, State Library and Archives, Nashville.

Lindsley, Dr. J. Berrien. "Cholera in Tennessee in 1833." Paper read at State Medical Society, April, 1888.

Nashville Journal of Medicine and Surgery, 1851. Also June, 1874, edition, Bowling, Dr. W. K., editor.

Nashville Union and American, June 1, 1873. Announcement of cholera epidemic by city physician. Also cholera stories on June 7, 1873; June 10, 1873; June 20, 1873; June 21, 1873.

Old City Cemetery Records, Nashville, 1849 to 1866.

Rosenberg, Charles F. *The Cholera Years in the U.S., 1832, 1849, 1866.* Chicago: University of Chicago Press, 1962.

Transylvania Journal, 1831. Transylvania University, Lexington, Ky.

Vandeman, Dr. J. H. "Cholera As It Appeared in State of Tennessee During Summer of 1873." Transylvania Medical Society 1875 XLVII, pp. 59–65.

Wood, Dr. B. "Cholera in Summer of 1853." *Southern Journal of Medical and Physical Sciences.*

Woodworth, Dr. John. "Cholera Epidemic in 1873 in the U.S." Surgeon-General's Office.

Yandell, Dr. Henry. "On Cholera in Shelbyville in 1833." *The Transylvania Journal of Medicine,* Lexington, Ky., 1834.

The Battle of Nashville

Beard, William E. *The Battle of Nashville; Including an Outline of the Stirring Events Occurring in One of the Most Notable Movements of the Civil War —Hood's Invasion of Tennessee.* Nashville: Marshall & Bruce, 1913.

Beasley, Paul. Interview with author, and tour of battleground, 1964.

"Hood's Nashville Campaign." *Civil War Times Illustrated,* December, 1964.

Horn, Stanley F. *The Decisive Battle of Nashville.* Baton Rouge: Louisiana State University Press, 1956.

Lawrence, J. S. Maps and deeds showing pivotal points in battlefield. Nashville. 1964.

Nashville American. Firsthand accounts of battle written on 25th anniversary. December 15, 1889.

Nashville Tennessean Special Edition. December 15, 1964.

Stokes, Walter, Jr. Interview by author about Battle of Nashville artifacts along Hillsboro Road, 1964.

Nashville's Biggest Party

Brown, Neill S. Interview by author about his grandfather, Eugene C. Lewis, 1965.

Centennial News. Published on Centennial grounds from January 4, 1896 to fall of 1897.

Chicago Times-Herald Centennial Edition. April 29, 1897.

Frazer, Mrs. James S. Interview by author about her father, Eugene C. Lewis, 1958.

Justi, Herman. *Official History of the Tennessee Centennial Exposition, Opened May 1 and Closed October 31, 1897.* Nashville: Brandon Press, 1898.

Killebrew, Joseph B. Speech to state legislature urging funds for Centennial celebration. J. B. Killebrew Papers. Manuscript Section, Tennessee State Library and Archives.

Minutes of meetings of Centennial Committee. Manuscript Section, Tennessee State Library and Archives.

Souvenir Book of the Tennessee Centennial, published by Brooklyn Party and New York State Commission to attend Nashville Exposition, October 8 to 15, 1897.

Tennessee Centennial and International Exposition. *Art Album of the Tennessee Centennial and International Exposition, Held in Nashville, May 1, 1897 to October 31, 1897.* Nashville: Marshall & Bruce Co., 1898.

————. *Commemoration of the One Hundredth Anniversary of Tennessee's Admission into the American Union.* Nashville: W. S. Rainey & Co., 1896.

————. *Official Catalogue of the Tennessee Centennial and International Exposition, Nashville, Tenn., May 1 to October 31, 1897.* Nashville, 1897.

————. *Woman's Department Catalogue,* May 1 to October 1, 1897. Nashville, 1897.

Wilted Roses versus Woman's Vote

Pearson, Josephine. Josephine Pearson Papers, including correspondence, speeches, clippings, memoirs. Manuscript Section, Tennessee State Library and Archives.

The Nashville Banner. Stories and editorials about special session of legislature to consider Woman's Suffrage. August 11 to September 4, 1920.

The Nashville Tennessean. Stories and editorials about special session of legislature to consider Woman's Suffrage. August 11 to September 4, 1920.

The Woman Patriot. Washington, D.C.: The Woman Patriot Publishing Co., September 11, 1920.

All Aboard for Union Station

Burt, Jesse C. *Nashville, Its Life and Times.* Nashville: Tennessee Book Company, 1959.

Clark, Blanche Henry. "Shifting Residential Patterns of Nashville." *Tennessee Historical Quarterly,* March, 1959.

Folmsbee, Stanley J.; Corlew, Robert E.; and Mitchell, Enoch L. *Tennessee, A Short History.* Knoxville: University of Tennessee Press, 1969.

Hackworth, W. S. *Over a Century of Railroad Service.* Paper given before Round Table Club of Nashville, March 26, 1953.

Interviews by author with railroad executives of N. C. & St. L. and others involved in Nashville train development, including: Morris Mashburn; W. Ovid Collins: Dan M. Wear; Sam G. Doak; Mrs. Sam G. Doak; Mrs. Louise G. Hall; Paul H. Beasley; Mrs. H. C. Brearley; James McCanless; James G. Stahlman; Bob Longhurst; Miss Lucy Dye; Mrs. Betty Gossett; and A. G. Adams.

Nashville American. Stories about opening of Union Station. October 9, 1900.

Waller, William, ed. *Nashville in the 1890s.* Nashville: Vanderbilt University Press, 1970.

————. *Nashville, 1900 to 1910.* Nashville: Vanderbilt University Press, 1972.

Index

209